THE AMATEUR PILOT

THE AMATEUR PILOT

John E. Milligan

CORNELL MARITIME PRESS
Centreville, Maryland

Library of Congress Cataloging in Publication Data

Milligan, John E., 1913–
The amateur pilot.

Includes index.
1. Seamanship. 2. Navigation. I. Title.
GV777.5.M54 623.88 81-19419
ISBN 0-87033-280-5 AACR2

Manufactured in the United States of America
First edition

CONTENTS

NOTE TO THE READER

FOR SIMPLICITY in indexing and for accuracy in making cross-reference, material is divided first into chapters in the usual manner, then further divided into subsections which are called articles. These are numbered consecutively through the book and are referred to by article number.

Figures are also numbered consecutively through the text. Tables, on the other hand, are located in an appendix in the back of the book, beginning with an explanation of them on page 110.

THE
AMATEUR PILOT

INTRODUCTION

THE EVENING could not have been more beautiful. The upper limb of the sun had just dropped below the horizon, and the green flash had been there. They had all seen it. The sky ahead under the broken overcast was a brilliant band of color with a central point of bright hot orange off the starboard bow where the sun had just set. On both sides the colors changed through washes of all the reds and into deep burgundy on either beam. Overhead, through the breaks in the low gray cloud cover, wisps of cirrus painted delicate strokes of magenta against the dark blue sky. The spray from the bow sparkled pink in the evening light as *Sea Breeze* surfed down each wave and plowed into the backwash of the one ahead.

The crew was jubilant. Their noon position had placed them at latitude 21°43′ N. longitude 155°07′ W., only ninety-two miles from the finish line off Kaanapali, Maui. Now, at sundown, they had only some forty miles to go.

Maui radio foretold of certain victory. The early leaders, all larger yachts with smaller handicaps, were in. *Sea Breeze* had until 0612 the following morning for a finish that would bring home all the silver. At her present fast pace her navigator had just given an ETA (estimated time of arrival) of five minutes past midnight.

The crew was alert, though tired. It had been a grueling two weeks, with 2,200 miles of hard racing since the start off Victoria, British Columbia, but there would be no sleep tonight. The pitch of excitement was too high. The taste of the anticipated champagne was already on everyone's lips.

The galley crew dug out the best that was left in the larder and prepared a sumptuous dinner of beef stew from a can and twice-baked bread. It was washed down with pineapple juice saved for the occasion. With dinner finished the eight man crew settled down in the cockpit swapping yarns of their adventure to date, while keeping a careful eye on the horizon ahead and watching for those west Maui mountains to pop up out of the gathering darkness.

The navigator examined the sky. Only an occasional star peeped through the overcast. He went below, checked the chart, and brought his estimated position up to the moment. It was 2000 local time. Thirty-two miles to go. "An evening star fix would be nice," he thought, "but it would be difficult to get through those clouds. We don't really need one," he concluded; noon positions had been dropping right on their DR (Dead Reckoning) for the past several days. A gibbous moon would rise a little before 2300 which would lighten the sky enough to see the mountains, and thus guide them into the seven mile wide channel between Maui and Molokai.

Nakalele light, flashing every two and a half seconds and marking the eastern edge of the channel, showed a range of only seven miles visibility. He wouldn't see it until the last hour, but that should be no problem. He called to the helmsman, "Hold her at 230°, right down the channel."

As with all navigators just before landfall on the strange shore, there was a nagging doubt in the back of his mind. "Have I done all that was necessary?" "No," he thought. "I could take another RDF (radio direction finder) bearing on Makapuu." (Makapuu radio on the island of Oahu was still there at the time. It would be removed for economy reasons by the end of the year.)

He tuned in the set. Since they were yawing so badly in the following sea with the chute up, he called the helmsman to give him a "mark" when the compass was on the ordered heading. The mark came, and Makapuu was still there at approximately 30° to starboard where it belonged.

There was nothing left to do now but wait for the mountains and the light to show. He gave his report to the skipper and stretched out on a handy bunk for a little rest before the final approach to the finish.

The hands slowly crept around the clock. Past nine. Past ten. Finally at an hour before midnight the moon poked its half round face above the cloud bank along the horizon astern and the sky brightened a bit.

"Mountains ahead," called a lookout.

The navigator and the skipper rushed forward to the mast to get a better look under the spinnaker. Ahead the clouds had broken a little and the rugged crest of mountains could barely be distinguished against the sky. The navigator lingered for some time searching to the right of the mountain silhouette for a sign of the Nakalele light. A half hour passed and finally came a dim flash, then it was gone.

"Come right 15°," he called to the helm. "We're heading to the left of the channel." He continued to watch and the flash came again. "We're further out than I thought," he mused. "The light is still hidden by the waves except when we are on top of one."

Excitement grew again, but the dim distant light seemed almost stationary. The flashes appeared only infrequently. It was three hours after midnight before the regular ten-second flash of the light brought about a quick dash back to the chart.

Sea Breeze was by then fifteen miles down the Molokai coast beyond the channel entrance to the finish line. It would be another mile before the chute was down, a small headsail was up, and they were beating back against the trade wind seas toward the finish.

The sad end to this story, which is only part fiction, is that a finish was finally made at mid-morning, well after the 0612 deadline. The mountains had not been West Maui, but East

Molokai. The light had been Makanalua on Kalaupapa Peninsula twenty miles down the Molokai coast. Its range of visibility is twenty-one miles.

The navigator of *Sea Breeze* (not her real name) was mortified. After the finish he sat glumly at his station seeking an explanation for his humiliating performance.

"Could he have done more?" The answer came back, yes.

Let's have a closer look at what might have taken place. First, and perhaps foremost, a closer examination of the chart would have shown mountains on both sides of the channel. The approach to a strange landfall should have included a planned error to the left, not to the center of the channel. This would have assured better identification of the mountains and allowed for which way to turn to reach the channel. *Sea Breeze* would have still been upwind with all racing sails pulling for the finish.

A closer examination of the pilot chart would have shown generally westerly, but somewhat confused, currents in the area *Sea Breeze* passed through during the several days before landfall. The currents are a steady westerly pattern in the last hundred miles. This could have been anticipated.

All lights in the area of the approach should have been identified on the chart, and their characteristics noted. With the seven mile range of Nakalele and the twenty-one mile range of Makanalua, the ranges almost overlap. The final identification of lights was too long in coming.

A cross bearing should have been made. It would have shown them well down the track and to the right of the channel. The chart shows a commercial radio station near the shoreline on Maui at a good angle from Makapuu radio. Although, as you will learn commercial radio is not the best for a RDF (radio direction finder), under some conditions, however, it can be used. Those conditions existed at the time a bearing was taken on Makapuu.

A greater effort might have been exerted to obtain an evening star fix. It should have been possible to sight at least two stars through the broken cover. Celestial navigation is another subject, however, and here we are dealing with piloting. Yes, they could have won with better piloting.

I was recently discussing a book I had written on celestial navigation, *Celestial Navigation by H.O. 249* (Cornell Maritime Press), with a friend at the yacht club. He remarked, "Oh I'm glad you did that, I never did know what all those buoys meant."

My friend is a person who has sailed his own boat for a good many years in Island waters. Unfortunately, he is representative of the many sailors who have taken the problems involved in piloting far too casually. We lose some of these sailors and their boats occasionally, but this loss could be avoided with a little more effort.

To those of you who do know, it is clear that buoys serve the pilot, not the celestial navigator. Celestial navigation does one thing. It provides you with a means of finding out where you are at a particular moment in time. But, by my definition, getting from where you are to where you want to be is primarily a problem in piloting.

I have another friend who clips out and saves articles that will be an aid to him in his sailing. He keeps them in a folder and takes them with him for handly reference when he goes on a sailing adventure. This is a part of his joy in sailing.

Let me emphasize that becoming a good pilot may require a little study, but the effort is part of the joy and being a good pilot is rewarding.

Increasing your fun and making your boating more enjoyable is also what this book is about. It is not intended to replace the more complete works on all aspects of seamanship that are available and used by many sailors. Its purpose is to serve as a handy reference. It is intended for the beginner who wants to start learning the skills of his hobby, or for the more experienced sailor who has been treating piloting too casually and is ready to improve his skills. I hope the use of this book will lead to a desire to possess a more complete work such as the *American Merchant Seaman's Manual,* (Cornell Maritime Press), or Bowditch to which I refer frequently.

1

DEFINITIONS

YOU NEED to become familiar with certain terms before you can advance your understanding of this text and become a skillful amateur pilot. These basic definitions and the minor ones that are treated as they come up in the text are as follows:

1. NAVIGATION

This term is used to refer to the entire process of directing the movement of a vessel or craft of any kind from one place to another. It is frequently used with words indicating the kind of craft, such as "air navigation," and the kind of medium over which it is conducted, such as "land navigation." It may also be used to indicate a segment of the process of navigation such as "celestial navigation."

2. PILOTING

Navigation which involves frequent determination of position by reference to terrestial objects or phenomena is called piloting. *Pilot waters* is a reference to coastal waters, harbors, rivers, and to other areas where, because of nearness to land or other traffic, a constant or near constant awareness of position is required to avoid danger. Directing the movement of a boat from celestial fix to celestial fix in the open ocean away from land or other traffic can be a much more casual operation then directing it in pilot waters. This is also treated as piloting, however, because attention to direction and distance, and to the possibility of other traffic, is still required even though to a lesser degree.

3. COURSE

The intended direction of travel (Fig. 1) is called course, and it may be measured in degrees from 000° (north) (art. 27) or by points of the compass (art. 26).

4. COURSE MADE GOOD

This is the single resultant direction from the point of departure to the point of arrival at any given time. It may differ from planned course because of current or leeway (art. 67), or even because of bad helmsmanship (Fig. 1).

5. TRACK

This is the route followed, the actual route (track) made in making good a particular course (Fig. 1). It may zigzag along the way or may deviate from course to avoid traffic for periods of time.

6. OVER THE BOTTOM

This can refer either to course or to track. It is a measure of both distance and direction made good by reference to the bottom of the ocean which is presumed to remain stationary and in a constant relationship to land.

7. DEAD RECKONING (DR)

This is the determination of position by advancing from a known position taking into account direction and distance

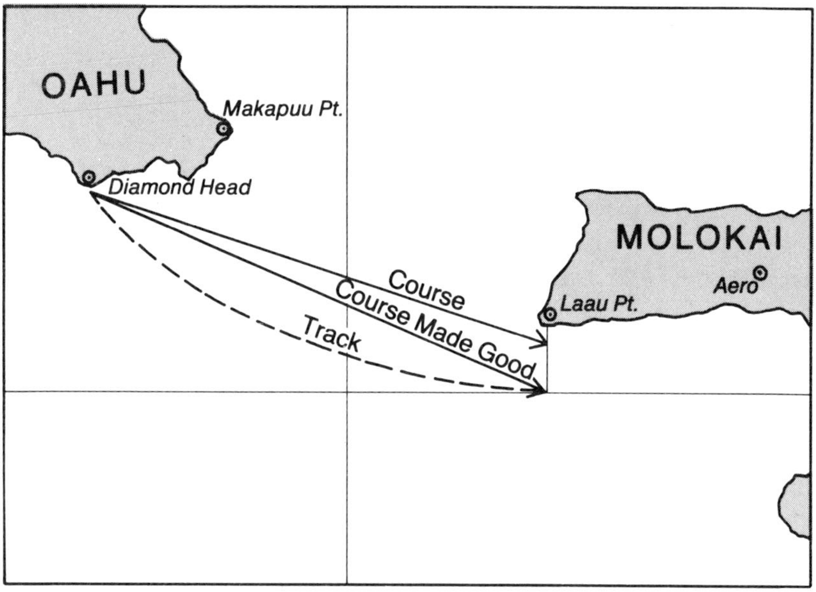
OAHU
Makapuu Pt.
Diamond Head
MOLOKAI
Aero
Laau Pt.
Course
Course Made Good
Track

Figure 1

through the water. It is frequently confused with estimated position.

8. ESTIMATED POSITION (EP)

This is a position taking into account all data known including distance and direction through the water as well as current, or leeway, or any other data which may be questionable as to accuracy. If DR and EP are kept separately, current or leeway can be inferred from the difference between the two.

9. FIX

This is a relatively accurate position determination which is made without reference to former positions.

10. BEACON

This is a fixed or stationary aid to navigation which provides a warning of danger or gives guidance to the sailor.

11. BUOY

This is a floating object (not a light ship) moored to the bottom to serve as an aid to navigation. It may be combined with a light or an auditory signal.

12. HEADING

This is the direction in which a boat is pointed or headed regardless of direction being made good.

13. RHUMB LINE

This is a line which intersects each meridian it crosses at the same angle. It appears as a straight line on a Mercator projection (art. 36), but it is not the shortest distance between two points (Fig. 2).

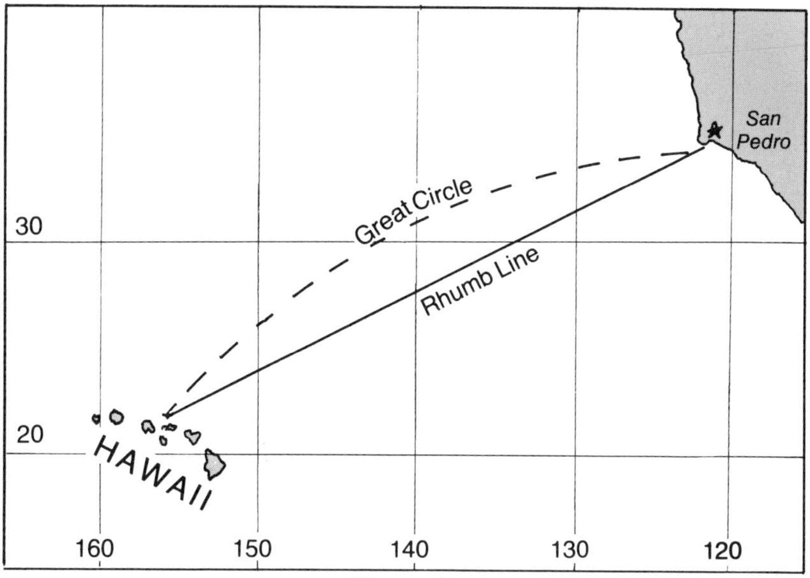
San
Pedro
Great Circle
Rhumb Line
30
20
HAWAII
160
150
140
130
120

Figure 2

14. GREAT CIRCLE

This is the shortest distance between two points on the surface of a sphere. A *great circle course* if extended around the earth would divide the earth in half. It appears as a curved line on a Mercator projection with the curve concave toward the equator, unless it is at the equator or along a meridian. All meridians (longitude lines) are great circles as is the equator. Parallels of latitude other than the equator are *small circles* (Fig. 2).

2

WHAT YOU WILL NEED

WHAT YOU will really need aboard for satisfactory piloting will depend in large part on the capability of your boat and where you plan to go. If you only sail within a familiar harbor in daylight, a good eye and a steady hand on the wheel or tiller are probably sufficient. If you plan to sail out of sight of land for extended periods you will need capability, certain publications, and specific equipment for celestial navigation. For the purposes of this manual assume that you will be sailing along a coast, between islands, or in other situations where land will be in sight most of the time except at night or when fog or other adverse weather conditions reduce visibility. For this you will need a good compass, one properly compensated with an up-to-date deviation card (see Chapter V). You will also need the following:

15. HAND BEARING COMPASS

This should be tested on the boat for deviation (art. 31). You can do this by sighting objects from a known position, reading the bearings, and then comparing the reading by referring to a chart showing the known position and the object or objects. Correction must be made for variation (art. 30), and the compass should be checked at each cardinal and intercardinal direction (art. 26).

16. CHARTS

These should cover the planned range of travel in small scale (large area) and large scale of the ports where you will call, as well as other areas where careful piloting will be required such as narrows, shoals, or areas congested with traffic.

17. PROTRACTOR

This is a device for measuring angles (Fig. 3). In this figure a course line from Diamond Head to the south point of the island of Lanai is being measured. The center of the protractor is placed at a convenient point where the course crosses a marked parallel of latitude. This line indicates true east and west (90°–270°) (Chapter III). To the right on the chart represents east, or 90°. The protractor shows that the course line is 33° beyond this, or 123° true.

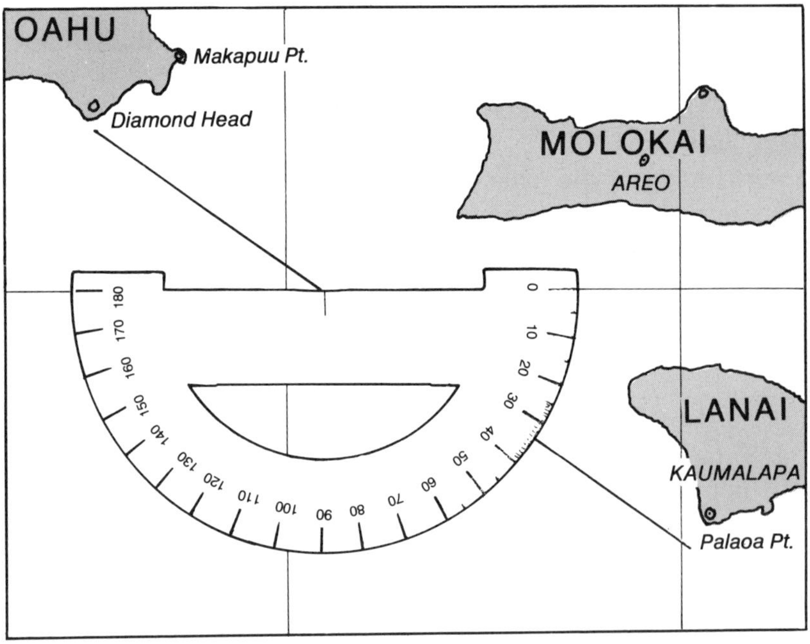

Figure 3

18. DIVIDERS

These are for measuring distance (Fig. 4). In this illustration a pair of dividers is shown measuring the mileage from Newport Beach, California to the west end of Catalina.

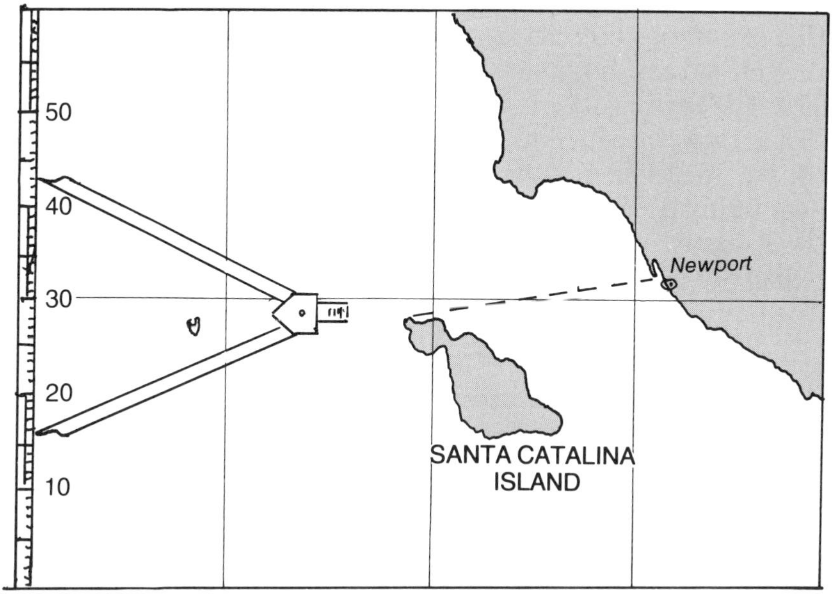

Figure 4

19. PARALLEL RULE

This is a device for moving a line of position and keeping it parallel with the original line, or for determining a course line or otherwise making comparisons with a compass rose on a chart (Fig. 5). In this illustration it is being used to advance a line of position (art. 66) along a course line. The parallel rule is first closed and aligned with a bearing line from a light house. The rule is in two parts labeled A and B. The distance traveled to the time for which the advance is made is marked off on the course line. Side A of the rule is then held firm while the rule is opened until side B is at the mark indicating the distance run. If the distance is greater than the span of the rule, the rule can be walked to position by holding firm first one side then the other. The advanced position line is then marked and labeled.

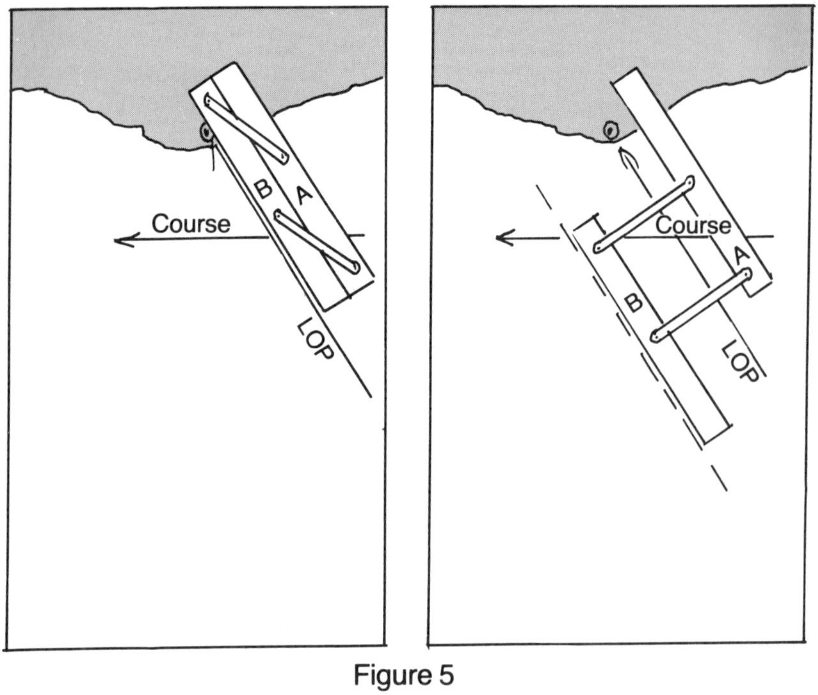

Figure 5

20. DRAFTING COMPASS

This instrument is much like a pair of dividers except that it has a pencil in one leg. It can be used for drafting a circle of position, or for measuring and marking in one action. It can substitute for dividers.

21. SPEED MEASURING DEVICE

If you wish to pilot your boat accurately, you will need some means of measuring speed through the water. There are a number of different types of knotmeters on the market today and most are not too expensive. If you have one it will no doubt need to be checked occasionally which can be done by locating or contriving a measured nautical mile and by making a series of runs at different speeds while timing the runs. To counteract the effect of current on the measured course, a run should be made in each direction and the time for the two runs averaged. Table I (see Appendix) gives you speed for times from 1 minute, 60 knots, to 13 minutes, 4.615 knots.

Many power boatmen use RPM (revolutions per minute) as a means of determining speed. The speed on the measured run is determined by trial at each of several power settings and a curve is then drawn through the various speeds obtained at each setting.

22. RADIO DIRECTION FINDER (RDF)

See Chapter X.

23. DEPTH MEASUREMENT DEVICE

A fathometer is not only nice to have, it is sometimes downright necessary. In the absence of such an instrument a hand lead line should be aboard when entering waters where depth is questionable. Depending on the circumstances surrounding your cruise, there are a number of publications and documents that you should have aboard. They include Light Lists, Tide Tables, among others and will be discussed as the appropriate subjects appear in the following chapters.

3

LATITUDE AND LONGITUDE

NAVIGATION HAS BEEN DEFINED as the process of directing the movement of a craft from one point to another on the globe. To do this with a degree of certainty we need a system of reference points. To establish these the surface of the earth has been divided into an imaginary grid of lines, some running north and south, others running east and west. Let's look at a simple grid and see how it works (Fig. 6). The vertical lines in this illustration are labeled 1 through 5 and the horizontal lines A through E.

We can locate the square in this example by the grid coordinates 1-B. The circle is at 3-C and the triangle at 4-E. To locate the X we will have to divide the grid into finer segments. In this case I have divided each major segment into ten sub-segments and numbered them .1 through .9. We can now locate the X by the coordinates 4.5 – B.5.

A grid of this type is frequently used in city maps for indicating the location of streets or parks, etc. It is also used in polar navigation where the lines indicating longitude are converging on the pole so sharply that they become inappropriate for locating positions.

The imaginary grid over the surface of the earth becomes an actual grid on the surface of a chart. The vertical lines are labeled longitude, and the horizontal lines are called latitude.

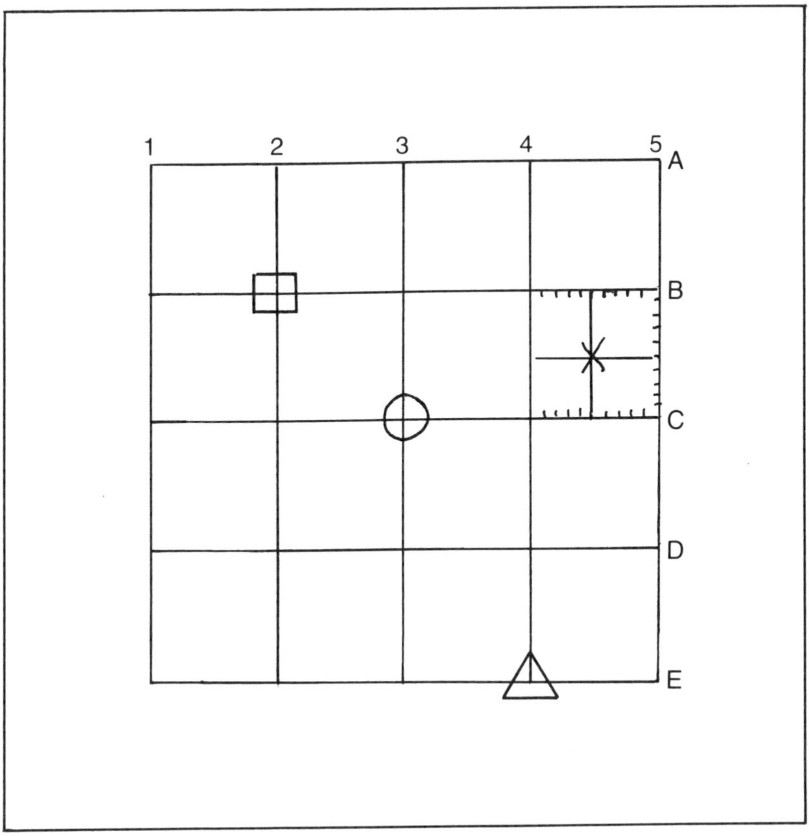

Figure 6

24. HOW LATITUDE IS PLOTTED

If you visualize the earth as an orange hanging in space from its stem end with its blossom end down, call the upper stem end north and the lower end south. Now, if you slice the orange in half crosswise exactly midway between the north and south ends you will have sliced it at its equator. The equator is zero degrees latitude.

If you next locate the very center of the orange (or the earth) and with a protractor measure from there upward at an angle of 10° from the center to the surface, mark, and then slice again parallel to the equator you will slice at 10° north latitude. If you measure downward in the same way and slice again parallel to the equator you will have sliced at 10° south latitude. You could measure and mark in this way for each degree of latitude up to 90°. The ninetieth degree, being perpendicular to the equator, would be only a point. These points mark the north and south geographic poles, the axis of the turning earth (Fig. 7).

As the earth is round (approximately) like a ball, it can be seen that each degree of latitude is going to be the same distance from its neighboring degree all the way from the equator to the poles. The earth is actually not perfectly round, it has some minor imperfections such as a bulge at the equator and some flattening at the poles, imperfections which you may ignore for purposes of this book. The earth being the size that it is, 1° of latitude is approximately sixty nautical miles. (A comparison of nautical and statute miles is provided in the Appendix, Table II.) Sixty nautical miles is a large distance for locating specific points on the surface of the earth. Therefore, each degree is subdivided into sixty segments. Each segment is equal to one minute of arc, or one nautical mile. The minute may again be divided into sixty subsegments, each being one second of arc, or one hundred feet. For convenience navigators frequently divide the minute into only ten parts and use the decimal system for indicating tenths. Twenty degrees, thirty and one half minutes, using the appropriate symbols would be written thus: 20° 30.5′.

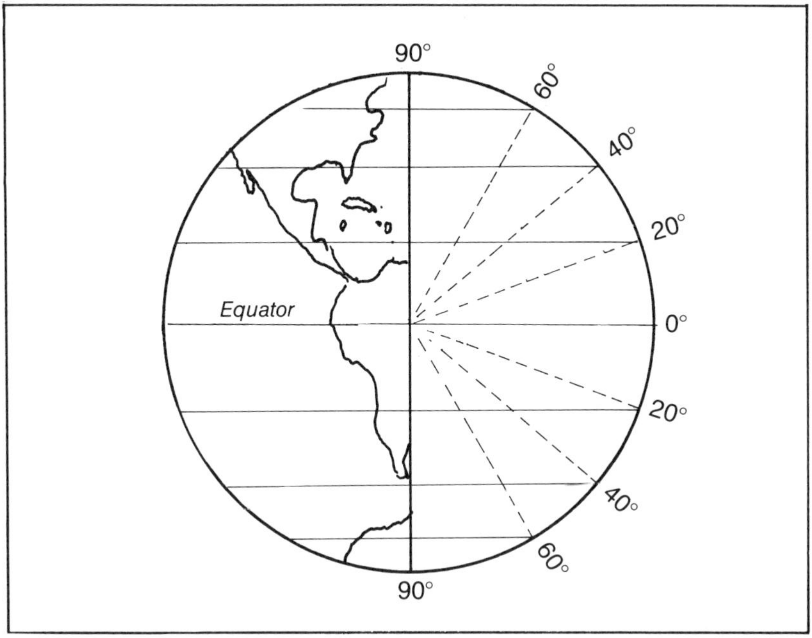

Figure 7

25. HOW LONGITUDE IS PLOTTED

Longitude is laid out quite differently from latitude, and again the orange provides a good illustration. If you peel an orange and take a good look at the lines separating the segments of the fruit you will see that all the lines start together at the stem end, run directly down around the fruit and meet again at the other end. The lines are farthest apart at the center, or equator (Fig. 8). Longitude lines on the surface of the earth run in exactly the same way.

If you cut the orange at the equator again you will see that the lines separating the segments come together in the center much like the lines separating pieces of pie after the pie has been cut. If you take a pie and make one cut from the center to the edge and then measure with a protractor an angle of 30° from that cut and then cut again you will have cut a piece of pie 30° wide. Longitude is measured in this manner. There are 360° in a circle. Therefore, there are 360° of longitude all the way around the earth. In labeling longitude however, you number in two directions from one point halfway until the numbering system meets at 180°. Those numbered toward the east from the starting point are called east longitude, those toward west are west longitude. The 180th degree is neither east nor west (Fig. 9).

It was simple dividing latitude at the midpoint between north and south, but it was not so simple finding a zero point for longitude. Throughout history a number of different points have been used by different peoples. At this time, however, everyone has pretty well agreed on a starting place. The imaginary line running from pole to pole and passing through a particular place in Greenwich, England is the prime meridian, or zero degrees longitude. East of Greenwich through 179° is east longitude, west of there is west longitude. The 180th degree (except where it deviates for special reason) is the internationally accepted date line, where Sunday becomes Monday when crossing from west longitude to east longitude, and Monday becomes Sunday when crossing back.

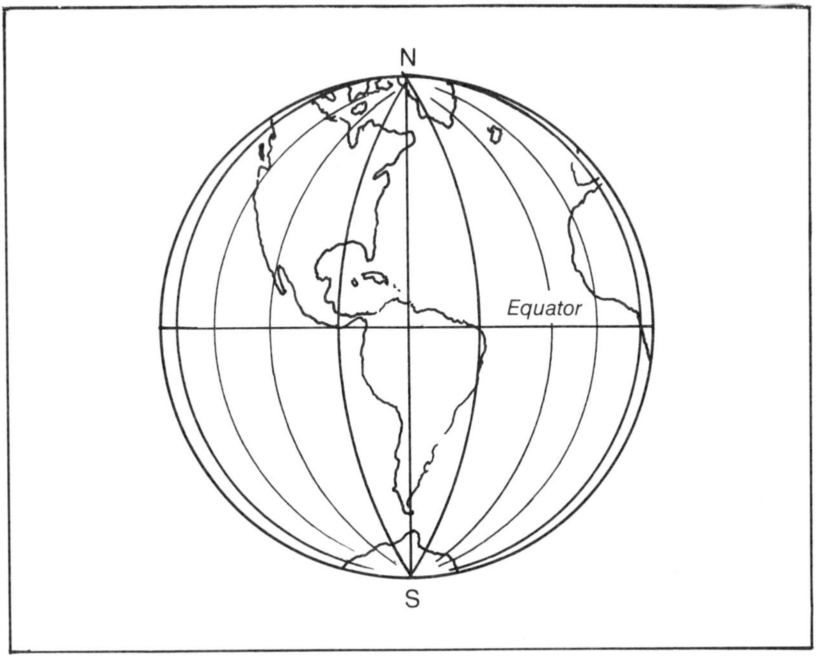

Figure 8

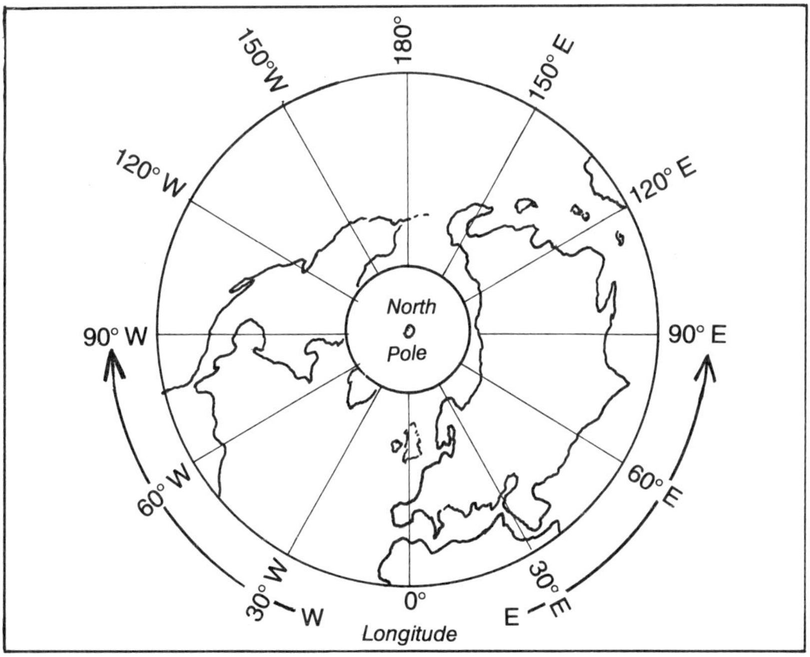

Figure 9

With all the degrees of longitude starting at one point at the poles, spreading apart at the equator, and coming together again at the opposite pole it is obvious that one degree of longitude cannot be equal to sixty nautical miles all over the globe. One degree of longitude does equal approximately sixty miles at the equator but toward the poles the distance constantly decreases until it is zero at the poles. This is important to remember when measuring distance on your chart. A chart is a flat surface which attempts to depict a portion of the earth's surface which is not flat, but round like a part of a ball. All charts have some error as a result (Chapter VI). U.S. Coast and Geodetic Survey charts used for ocean navigation are made by what is called the Mercator projection method (art. 36). On these charts lines of longitude are drawn parallel to each other and the distance between them therefore represents a lesser and lesser actual distance as one moves from the equator toward the poles. Thus, when measuring mileage on such a chart, measure the minutes of latitude (nautical miles) from the side of the chart at the latitude where the mileage is being measured. If a long distance north and south is being measured, a measurement taken from the mid-latitude will average out accurately for the entire distance.

4

REFERENCE DIRECTION

JUST TO BE SURE we understand what we are talking about let's start with a basic example. As I leave my home each morning and drive to the office I have no need for any specific direction reference other than perhaps right and left. If I were one of those people who have difficulty with right and left, I wouldn't even need that so long as I remembered to turn to the remembered way at the remembered corner. I have street signs to tell me the names of the streets. I have prominent buildings and other landmarks to remind me where I am while on the way. When I try to explain or illustrate to someone else how I get to my office, street names, prominent buildings, and right and left are convenient. Right and left, however, change in relation to the fixed pattern of the city. A right turn going to the office is a left turn going home. If I were to draw an illustration of my city (a map) and particularly, if I draw it as it is in relation to some other place, such as Pearl Harbor, I need some sort of fixed reference so that the relationship will be understandable.

My city, Honolulu, happens to be a rare one for this example. It is laid out, if I may use an old but expressive term, catawampously. The main through streets run a little off of north-west, southeast. Diamond Head is at one end of the city and out in the country opposite is the Ewa sugar plantation. By Island practice, directions toward these two ends are called

Diamond Head and Ewa. Across these through streets is the sea on one side and the mountains on the other. The Hawaiian terms for these two directions are Makai meaning toward the sea, and Mauka meaning toward the mountains. There may be many similar local expressions in other cities, but when map-makers lay out cities they will use a north-south, east-west orientation. In our every day lives within the city we may pay very little attention to north, south, east, and west. At sea there are no handy corners, no prominent buildings, no sign posts. There are aids to navigation however, and there is a pointer to north, the one major reference direction. From north we can find all other directions.

Getting from here, wherever here is, to there, wherever there may be, is a problem in direction and distance. Distance involves speed and time, and we will get to that; but for the moment let's stick to direction.

26. CARDINAL AND INTERCARDINAL DIRECTIONS

For various reasons north is the direction directly toward one axis of the turning earth chosen as the major reference direction. To examine the directions to be located from north, imagine you are standing in an open field. Around you is the whole circle of the horizon where the sky meets the land. You are facing north. To your right, one quarter of a circle clockwise, is east. Directly behind you, one quarter of a circle further, is south. West is to the left one quarter of a circle further. Continuing on around the last quarter circle, you are back to the way you were facing, or back again to north. These are the four cardinal directions.

Now start around the circle again, but this time note the points halfway between the four cardinal directions. The first is between north and east and this direction is called northeast. Your next stop is between east and south. Call this southeast. On around to the next stopping place you are at southwest, and finally halfway home from west you are at northwest. These are the intercardinal directions.

By dividing the circle into cardinal and intercardinal directions, I have divided it into eight parts. If I divide each arc, or part, in half and then divide each new part in half again I would have thirty-two named directions. Sailors used to, and some still do, refer to direction by using all these names and fractions thereof (Table III). If you were a boy or girl scout, you may have learned these names. It was called, "boxing the compass," and these names are referred to as the points of the compass.

27. DEGREES

Today most sailors, amateur and professional, use a simpler method of indicating direction. Mathematicians have divided the circle into three hundred sixty parts. These are called degrees, and they are numbered, for navigational purposes, clockwise from north. Look again at the four cardinal directions. Facing north at the beginning of the circle, number it zero. East is one quarter of the circle clockwise. One quarter of 360° is 90°; so east is at 90°. South is one quarter further at 180°. This will make west 270° and completing the circle of 360° you are back to north again. North may be referred to as either 360° or 000°. Note that I have used three zeros to indicate north. This is a usual practice among sailors. It is intended to avoid confusion. With this system, east would be referred to as 090°.

You will remember from earlier discussion (art. 24), the degree is divided into sixty minutes and the minute into sixty seconds. In piloting a small boat, except in absolutely ideal conditions, it is difficult to steer to an accuracy of one or two degrees, not to mention minutes. We will, therefore, seldom use anything finer than a degree in referring to direction.

In looking back at the thirty-two named directions and comparing them with degrees, you can determine with a little arithmetic that each named direction is eleven and one quarter degrees from its neighbor. That was not fine enough for accurate steering. Therefore, the named directions were divided further fractionally. To compare points with degrees see Table III (in the Appendix).

28. MAP AND CHART LAYOUT

By tradition, maps (primarily illustrations of land) and charts, (primarily illustrations of sea) are oriented so that north is at the top as you look at them. This makes east toward the right, south toward the bottom and west to the left. This tradition may not always be followed for maps or charts of small local areas, but when it is not, there will be an indication of north. From here all other directions can be determined by angular measurement (art. 27).

5

THE COMPASS

A LONG, LONG time ago a young Viking sat in a quiet glade by a small still pool of clear water working diligently to shape the iron battle-ax he would carry on his next venture across the North Sea with his fellow Vikings. As he worked his attention was attracted to tiny slivers of iron held suspended by the surface tension of the water in the pool. Curious, he thought, how they all appeared to form into lines pointing in the same direction. As he studied them further he noted that they all pointed toward that northern star that prescribed such a small circle in the sky. He couldn't, of course, see the star now in the bright sunlight. He knew exactly where it was, however, as did all his fellow Vikings, for it was this beacon which pointed the way home when they were returning from their distant adventures. His mind wandered as he worked, and he was taken back in memory to that last fearful voyage home when the sea was covered with a blanket of fog so thick that for days one could hardly see beyond the bow of the longboat. They had rowed and rowed not knowing for sure in what direction, as the sea remained flat and still, and the sky was hidden from view. Finally the breeze had come, and the chill white blanket had been blown away revealing the heavens. What a relief it had been finding that star again with its companions to point the way home.

He looked again at the bits of iron floating on the water. "Yes, it was very curious. Was there a message in this? Had no one else ever noticed this strange thing? Perhaps it was only being revealed to me." He wondered, "Would the bits of iron always form for me in this particular way?" If so, could he use them to point out the place of the northern star in the heavens even though it was hidden from view behind a blanket of fog?

He reached for his earthen mug and scooped up the bits of iron and the water that held them suspended, but, alas, with the movement of the water the bits all sank to the bottom of the mug. "Hmmm," he mused as he plucked a stalk of grass and chewed on the sweet tender end. "Would a larger needle of iron point to the star in the same manner? How could I float it on the water?" He plucked another stalk of grass and started to bite off the end.

"That was it," he thought, as he studied the stalk. He would break away a segment of the grass stalk, place a needle of iron inside, and then seal the open end with a dab of pitch from a nearby tree.

He worked carefully with a fire-hardened tool until he had cut away his small needle. He pierced the membrane at the end of the segment of grass and thrust the needle inside. He sealed the end and carefully placed the straw in the water-filled mug. He watched. Slowly, ever so slowly, the straw turned until it aligned itself with what we call Polaris or the north star. He turned it away and watched again. As before, it turned and was only still when it was pointing to the north.

Our young Norseman had just invented the first compass. This story is fiction, but it could very well be nearly true. We don't know who invented the magnetic compass; historians do not tell us. We do know, however, that early ocean travelers from the north used small needles of iron afloat in a straw to point the way home. There is also a claim that early Chinese sailors made the same discovery. We only know for sure that the magnetic compass has a long history with sailors of the seven seas.

The magnetic compass of today is very little changed from that bit of iron afloat within a straw. The bit of iron and the cup that holds it are more precisely made. The iron is normally attached to a card which swings with it and which numbers the points around the circle of the compass. The iron is still suspended in a liquid, but it is carefully balanced on a jeweled point to keep it centered in the compass bowl. It still points to the north, or nearly so, as we will learn.

29. MAGNETISM

Why does the needle of a compass point to the north? The answer lies in the mystery of magnetism, a phenomenon known for centuries! Magnetism is the attraction seen in pieces of iron which attract and hold other pieces or that discovered in lodestone, in which chunks of earth attract other chunks. Only recently have we learned the whys of this mystery. The fields of attraction in a magnetized piece of iron, around a wire carrying a direct current, and encircling the core of the earth are a result of the same force, that is the force holding the atom together. When the electrons in a substance are spinning around their nuclei all in the same plane, or are aligned with the spinning of other electrons around other nuclei in the substance, they create the attraction we call magnetism. When the planes of the spinning electrons are random, there is no magnetism. The direction of the plane can be changed by the introduction of a strong magnetic field in the substances. In some substances the plane of the spinning electrons will return to random as soon as the stronger field is removed. In others, it will remain as it was, aligned by the stronger field. This change in alignment happens mostly with iron, although it can happen with nickel, cobalt, silver, and to some extent with other metals. Iron of a type where the alignment returns to random after the field is removed is referred to as soft iron, that which holds its alignment is called hard iron. It is hard iron that forms permanent magnets.

A magnet will establish what we refer to as lines of force (Fig. 10). In this illustration the lines of force are characterized as entering one end of the magnet, exiting from the other end, and circling back around to re-enter at the first end. All magnets have these two ends. If a bar magnet is cut, each piece will be magnetized and each will have ends of this same character. The end where the lines of force enter is referred to as the south end or the blue end. The end where they exit is the north or red end. Magnets used in compasses usually have one or both ends painted to indicate which end is which.

Like ends of a magnet repel each other, unlike ends attract. In soft iron where magnetism is present only as a result of outside force fields, the ends of the magnet will change as the soft iron orientation is changed within the field. This is one of the problems with compasses in steel ships and in part, the cause of deviation (art. 31) in any boat that has magnetic metals in it.

The earth is somewhat like a great magnet. There is a north magnetic pole and a south magnetic pole. These poles, however, are not in line with the geographic poles. They are not even through the center of the earth. The north magnetic pole is at approximately 75° north latitude, 101° west longitude while the south magnetic pole is at approximately 67° south latitude, 142° east longitude. They are likewise not fixed and move around a bit from time to time (art. 30).

But, back to the compass. The magnetic compass worked for the young Viking because that sliver of iron in the straw had been magnetized and retained its magnetism. It aligned itself with the magnetic force field of the larger magnet, the earth. Compasses of today do exactly the same thing.

30. VARIATION

I have said that the compass points only approximately north. This is so in part because the magnetic poles are not at the geographic poles. Why the magnetic poles are off-center is not known, but it is presumed to be because of the distribution of

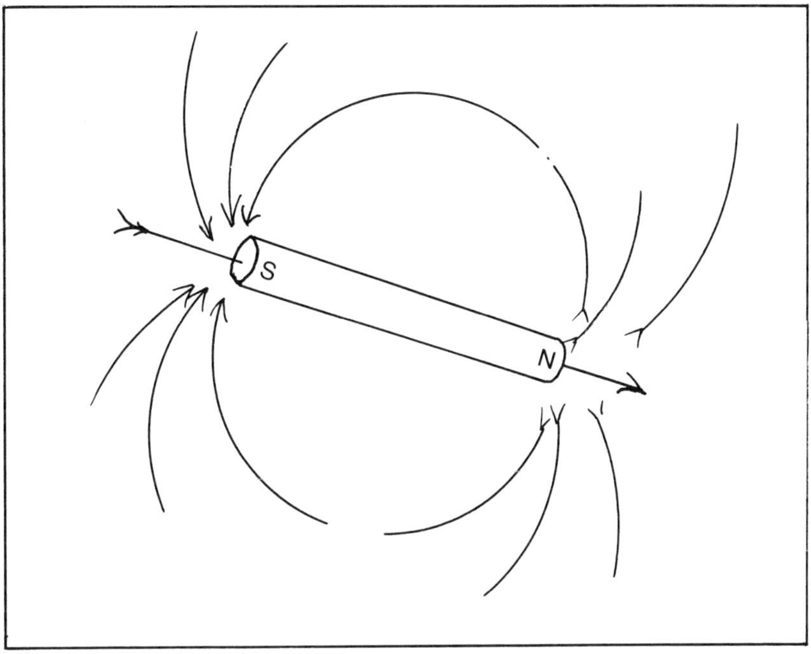

Figure 10

iron in the core of the earth. For whatever reason, our compasses do err, and this particular error is called variation. Variation changes for different locations on the earth. Variation can be visualized this way: if a compass is on a boat in the far north at the same latitude but to the east of the magnetic pole, it would point west toward the pole with an error of 90°. If it were south of the magnetic pole and on a line between the magnetic and geographic poles, there would be no error, and the variation would be zero. This example, I must point out, is oversimplified. The lines of force around the earth are not regular, they bend, turn, and wander. Lines of force causing variation actually change a bit during the day, but this change is so small it can be ignored in navigation. The annual change, however, must be considered. There are stations at many places around the world which keep track of this change and make their predictions of change available to chart makers.

While considering a boat in the far north, let me give this word of caution. Polar navigation is a separate problem in itself. The magnetic compass becomes weaker and weaker as it moves toward the pole. This is so because the lines of force are oriented more nearly in the vertical as one nears the pole, and thus have less and less lateral effect on the compass magnets which are held in the lateral plane. The effect is to make the compass want to dip and point down. There are also problems with a chart in polar areas. Remember, the lines of longitude are coming together at the geographic pole and thus, east and west become more and more meaningless. At the pole there is, of course, only one direction. From the north pole every direction is south. The opposite is true from the south pole.

If interested in polar navigation you should make a separate study of the problems to be encountered. Bowditch, *American Practical Navigator* H.O. Publication No. 9 is a good place to start. This book can be obtained from the U.S. Government Printing Office.

For most amateur pilots who sail in the temperate or tropic zones of the earth, variation will range from 0° to not over 25 to 30°. Your chart (Chapter VI) will give you the information you need to determine variation where you are. This information will be provided in one of two forms depending on the scale of your chart. On large area (small scale) charts, such as one of the Pacific or Atlantic oceans, there will be lines of equal variation across the face of the chart. Charts of smaller areas will have one or more compass roses (Fig. 11) on the chart. A compass rose, as you can see in this figure, is a circle within a circle. The outer circle will number the degrees around the compass from 000° at true north. The inner circle will number the degrees from magnetic north, and within the circle will be information on annual change in variation.

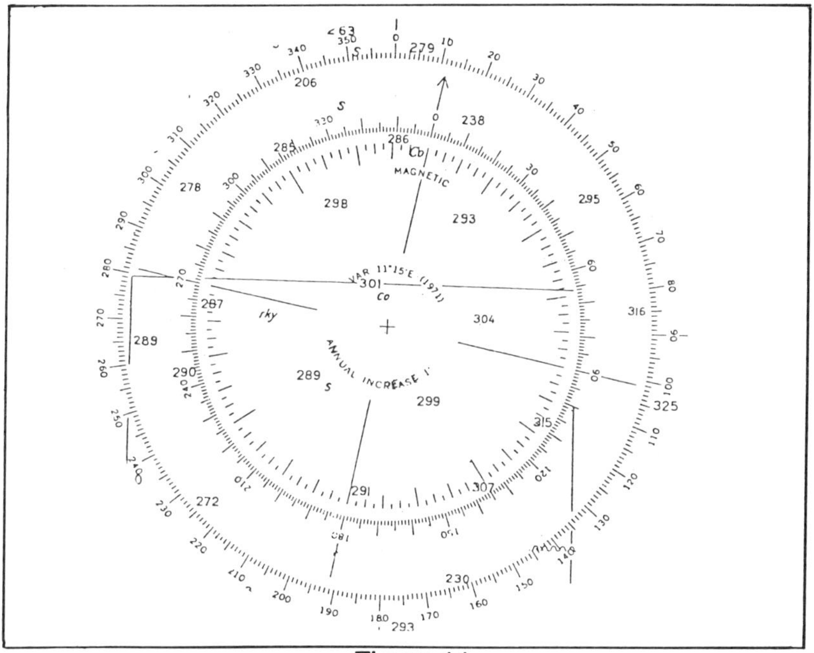

Figure 11

From this compass rose you can see immediately how variation affects a course as compared with true direction. The compass rose in Figure 11 is selected from a chart of my own home waters off Honolulu. The variation as you can see, is 11°15′east, or it was in 1971 when the chart was printed. The annual change is an increase of one minute per year.

You will note that variation is referred to as either east or west. This means that with east variation the north-pointing needle points toward the east from north. With west variation it varies toward the west from north. I find conversion formulas from true to magnetic or from magnetic to true, difficult to remember as mere formula. When converting either way in either direction, I visualize the compass rose and mentally read off the change. If, however, you are formula minded, use the following: From true to magnetic with easterly variation, subtract variation from true direction. From magnetic to true, add. From true to magnetic with westerly variation, add. From magnetic to true, subtract.

Here is an example: I am planning a cruise in this illustration (Fig. 12), from harbor A to island harbor B. With my protractor oriented so that the straight edge is along a convenient vertical (longitude), I measure the course at 270° true, due west. The compass rose on my chart indicates a variation of 11°15′ E. I can't steer to an accuracy of 15′. Therefore, I ignore it and consider it 11°. I can read the magnetic heading directly by placing a straight edge from the center of the compass rose to 270° on the outer circle and then reading the magnetic course from the smaller circle. The answer is 259°. I could get the same answer as easily by following the formula, true to magnetic with easterly variation, subtract 11° from 270° equals 259°. You will have more practice with this problem when you begin to plan your courses but, another compass error must also be understood.

31. DEVIATION

Remember the phenomenon of magnetism? Any ferrous metal, iron as well as some others, can have magnetic quality. Direct current running through wire can create magnetism. Your compass needle points to magnetic north because of the magnetic attraction of the earth. If there is an attraction within your boat that is strong enough, it will affect your compass and cause it to deviate from magnetic north. If your boat happens to

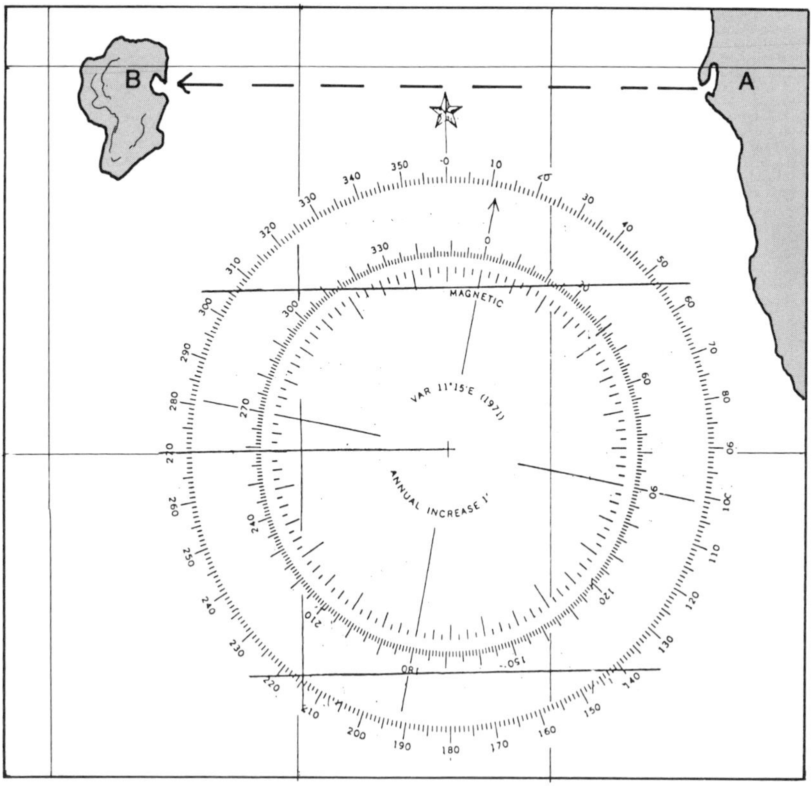

Figure 12

be steel, it will have a great deal of effect on your compass. Engines are made of ferrous metal, so are most tools, paint cans, beer cans, etc. The greater the bulk of the metal, or the nearer to the compass the greater the effect will be. Three or four feet between an engine and a compass is usually enough to reduce deviation to a manageable minimum. Tools and canned goods should be stowed away from the compass. Some wiring may be needed near a compass, but it should be kept to a minimum. When all possible care has been taken to protect your compass from stray magnetism, there will usually still be a bit left over. This is then the time to have your compass checked for deviation. If you want the best results, the job

HULA GAL IV
BRIDGE COMPASS

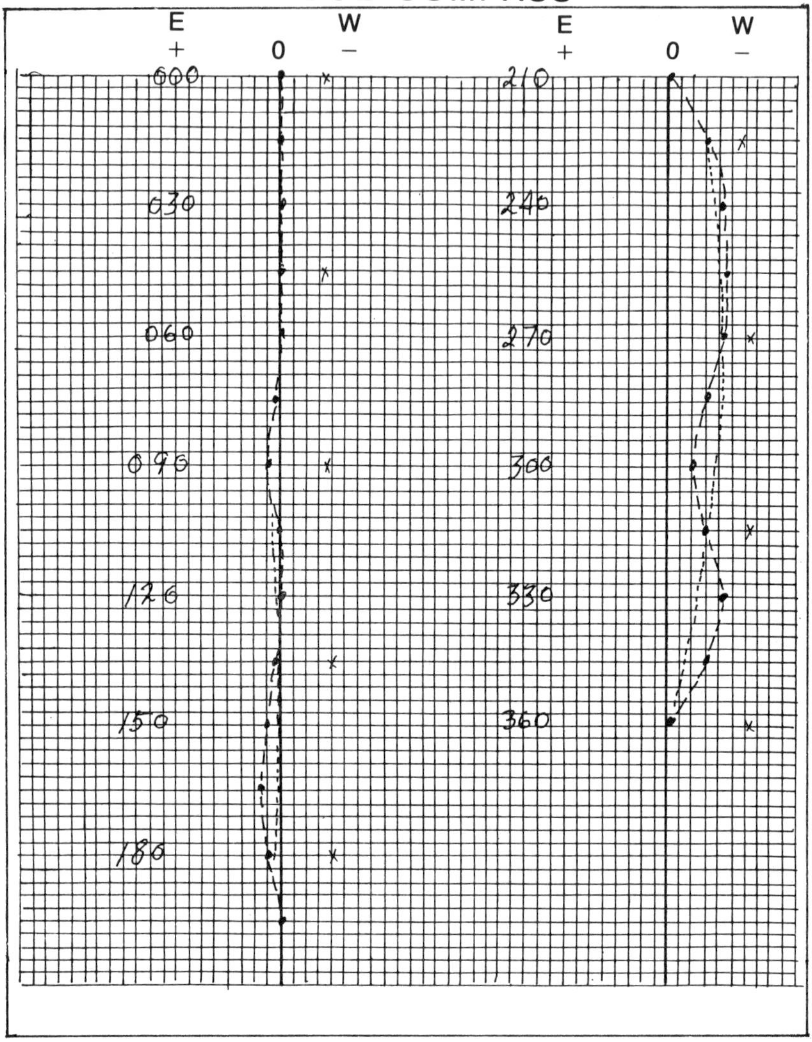

Figure 13

should be done by a professional. If your compass is a good one, it will be equipped with compensating magnets which can be manipulated by the specialist to reduce error. He will "swing the ship," that is, he will head the boat in every cardinal and intercardinal direction (or perhaps every 30°) and read the error by known reference. He will plot the error on graph paper (Fig. 13) and connect all plotted errors with a smooth curve. This will provide a reading of deviation at any point around the compass. He will then provide you with a card to post somewhere near your compass so that it will be handy for reference when you need it (Fig. 14).

Vessel- HULA GAL IV

Compass- BRIDGE

To Go	Head	To Go	Head
000	000	180	179
015	015	195	195
030	030	210	210
045	045	225	228
060	060	240	244
075	074	255	260
090	089	270	274
105	105	285	288
120	120	300	302
135	135	315	318
150	149	330	334
165	164	345	348

Date 7/15/74

By: John E. Milligan

Figure 14

It must be obvious by now that deviation is not the same on all headings. This is so because of soft iron in your boat and the fact that the relationship between your compass and the material affecting it changes as your boat changes headings. It must also be remembered that deviation changes as time passes, and if new stores and tools are added. If they are kept sufficiently away from the compass, they present no problem. But, new instruments may be added and other changes may be made which do affect the deviation. I would want to have my compass reswung before a long voyage with all stores aboard or after a major alteration. Bowditch suggests that steel ships should be reswung every three months. I would think that for a wood or fiberglass boat an annual check should be sufficient.

If you want to do the job yourself, and you may, particularly if you sail close to home, get out the chart of the area around your harbor. Locate a number of ranges (art. 62) that are easy to find from the sea. You can use radio towers, mountain peaks, or any prominent marks that are accurately located on your chart. Find a sufficient number that line up in pairs and provide as nearly as possible headings for the cardinal and intercardinal directions. Remember, you can use one pair for two headings, toward and away from the range. Once you have found them, compute their magnetic bearing and then run them. Be sure that the center line of the boat is in line with the range when you take the compass reading. You can then follow the method of the professional and plot your readings on graph paper, draw your curve, and prepare your own deviation card from the results. You should always have a few of these ranges in mind or recorded so that you can make periodic checks on your compass even if it was swung by an expert. If you have more than one compass on your boat, each must be swung separately as they will be in different environments.

32. DEVIATION CHANGE WITH LATITUDE

If you cruise extensively, you should be aware that deviation can change with latitude. For the mid-latitudes this is relatively unimportant for the average yachtsman, but if you sail over wide ranges, it should be taken into account. You will remember the tendency of the compass needle to dip and point down as one nears the magnetic pole. This situation causes a weakening in the lateral force of the earth's magnetic field and a relatively stronger effect by the forces in your boat causing deviation.

If you are planning a cruise of the world, whether in high latitudes (nearer the poles) or not, you should know how to check your compass by using the shadow from the sun. Such a cruise will require a knowledge of celestial navigation and from here to using the sun's shadow is a small step. The tables used in celestial navigation provide an easy reference to the azimuth of the sun for every minute of the day.

33. LOCAL DISTURBANCE

There are a number of natural magnetic irregularities around our globe. Notes on your chart will warn you of these, and you should look for such notes when sailing into strange waters. In addition to these natural areas, such things as large steel ships, large pieces of machinery, or electric current in close proximity can disturb your compass and cause it to deviate. Just remember the larger the mass and the nearer to your compass, the greater the effect will be. For an experiment take an ordinary steel screw driver, hold it next to your compass, and move it around while you watch the behavior of the compass.

I am reminded here of the time I was swinging a compass for a friend. The Ala Wai yacht harbor was being rebuilt in one area, and a good sized open space of water was left which appeared to be a nice smooth place to take the boat for the job at hand. I was about half finished when I noticed unexplainable irregularities creeping into my figures. Someone else was maneuvering the boat while I concentrated on the compass. I looked up and around, and there, not twenty feet away, was a very large metal pile driver. I got out of there, found another spot, and finished the job with no further troubles. I might have checked the area before I started, but it was a good lesson learned.

34. COMPASS INSTALLATION

If your compass was installed by the manufacturer, it should be properly aligned with the center line of your boat. You might check to be certain that it is so. If you are mounting your own compass, you must make sure that it is so aligned.

The marine compass has a line inscribed, or otherwise situated, on the inside of the compass bowl forward. This is called the "lubber's line." When your boat turns, this line remains aligned with your boat and the compass heading is read as the compass card swings by the line. The lubber's line and the center of the compass must be in line with the center line, the keel, of the boat if the compass is to give an accurate indication of heading. If the compass is the type that mounts on a bulkhead, then the bulkhead must be at right angles to the keel line, or suitable mounting correction must be made. If the bulkhead slopes aft, as so many do on sailboats, then a mounting correction to an upright position is required.

The keel line can usually be found easily by reference to a flagstaff, a mast, or by measuring to the center of the deck at various places. A taut string can then be strung down the center line to indicate keel line. The compass should be located conveniently to the helmsman in order that he can look across the center. Sailboats which are steered with a tiller frequently have a compass mounted on each side of the cockpit so that they will be properly oriented for the helmsman on either tack.

Sailboat compasses may differ from power boat compasses in two ways. They will be well gimballed so that they will remain upright while the boat is heeled, and they will often have auxiliary lubber's lines at 45° from the fore and aft line to help indicate the best angle for a tack when beating to windward.

35. SUMMARY

We now have three reference directions which we must keep in mind and make allowance for as the cruise progresses from day-to-day. They are:

True. The way globe is laid out geographically, and thus the way charts are laid out.
Magnetic. The direction compass will point aligning itself with the magnetic forces of the earth provided there is no interference.
Compass. The direction compass will actually point in boat's present condition.

True direction remains constant. Magnetic direction changes as variation changes with change in position in the earth's magnetic field. Compass direction remains reasonably constant on each heading so long as the compass environment remains unchanged.

When making chart notes in the process of navigating, we make a notation of the particular direction used. A single letter is normally used: T. for true; M. for magnetic; and C. for compass.

I have not tried to treat the problems encountered with a compass and a steel boat, and there are some steel boats sailed by amateurs. Compass deviation on such a yacht is a job for an expert, and I would suggest that you use one.

6

CHARTS

YOUR LIBRARY of charts and your compass comprise the most important aids you will have aboard for proper piloting. The nautical chart comes from a history as long as that of the compass, but again history is incomplete. The earliest charts cover relatively large areas, but, as it is easier to draw a picture or an illustration rather than explain how to get somewhere, it is reasonable to believe that the first cartographers used mariners' notes and illustrations as a base for their charts. Early charts were quite picturesque and fanciful. Later as sailors brought home more and more information, charts improved and became more accurate and factual. The chart of today is a very complete document illustrating what man has learned over the centuries about the sea and the lands at journey's end.

Cartographers have always found it difficult to portray accurately the round surface of the earth on a flat piece of parchment or paper. It is still difficult, and all reproductions of the earth's surface, except on a globe, must make allowance in some form for this problem. All charts have some error when compared with the actual surface of the earth.

36. MERCATOR PROJECTION

There are a number of methods of projecting a portion of the surface of the earth on a flat surface. The one most used by mariners is the Mercator projection named after the Flemish geographer who devised it in the sixteenth century. The Mercator chart is a cylindrical projection, and although it is constructed according to a mathematical formula which takes into account the irregularities in the shape of the earth, its form can best be visualized by the following example. If I had a transparent globe of the earth with latitude, longitude, and the continents drawn on it, and if I placed a bright pinpoint light at the center of the globe and a cylinder of paper around the globe (Fig. 15a), the light would project the shadow of the lines on the

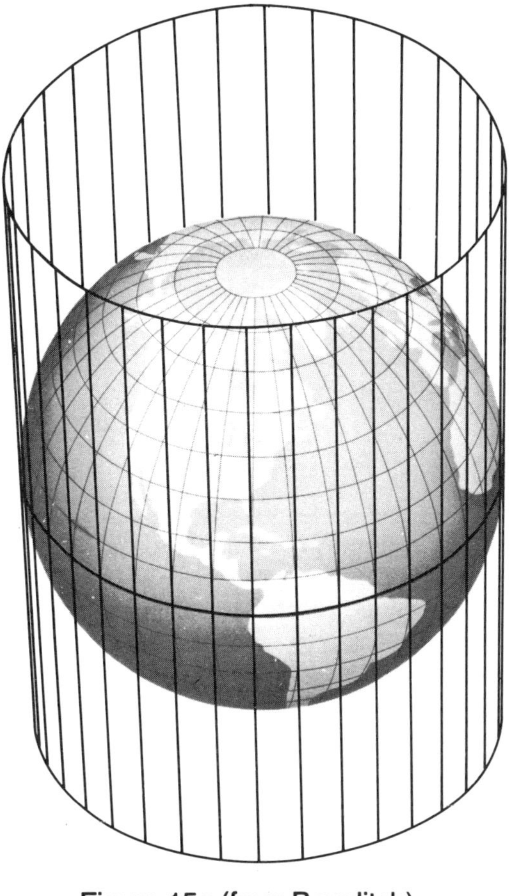

Figure 15a (from Bowditch)

paper. If I then cut the paper at a convenient place and laid it out flat, I would have an approximation of a Mercator map of the world (Fig. 15b). In this illustration the equator would be the point of tangency because it is where the cylinder is tangent to the globe. By examining the illustration, you can see accuracy is only apparent near the equator at this point of tangency. Expansion of the parallels of latitude is obvious as one approaches the poles. The poles and the area adjacent to them cannot be portrayed at all as expansion reaches infinity at the poles. Meridians (lines portraying longitude) appear as parallel vertical lines.

The cylinder of the cylindrical projection need not necessarily be made tangent to the equator. It can be made tangent at any part of the globe and frequently is for airway strip maps, polar charts, and for other special purposes. The true Mercator chart is made from mathematical tables which take into ac-

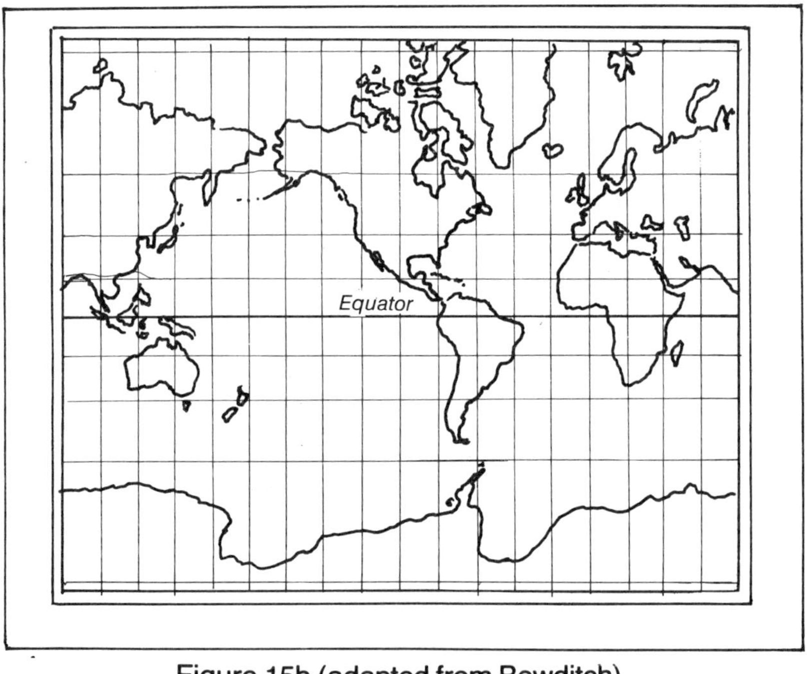

Figure 15b (adapted from Bowditch)

count the flattening of the earth at the poles and the bulge around the equator. The true Mercator chart also provides for consistent expansion throughout the area of the chart. Because of this expansion, mileage cannot be measured from a single scale except for charts of small areas where expansion is insignificant. The latitude scale at the side of the chart where mileage is being measured gives an accurate measurement. Remember, one minute of latitude equals one nautical mile.

There are a number of different projections used for maps and charts, each serving a particular purpose. Bowditch covers this subject thoroughly. I will discuss a few that you may find useful in marine navigation.

37. CONICAL PROJECTION

With this projection a simple cone is presumed to be placed over the globe and projection from the center of the globe made against this cone (Fig. 16). This reduces error somewhat toward the pole but is still accurate only at the point of tangency where the cone touches the globe. There are a number of variations on the conical theme, the most popular being the polyconical. With this a series of cones is used, each providing surface for projection of a narrow band of the earth (Fig. 17).

38. LAMBERT CONFORMAL

With this modification of the polyconical the spacing along the parallels is altered so that the distortion along them is the same as along the meridians. A straight line on a Lambert conformal is very nearly a great circle. In appearance this projection is much like a simple conic.

39. GNOMONIC PROJECTION

If a plane flat surface is placed tangent to the globe, and a projection is made from the center of the globe against the

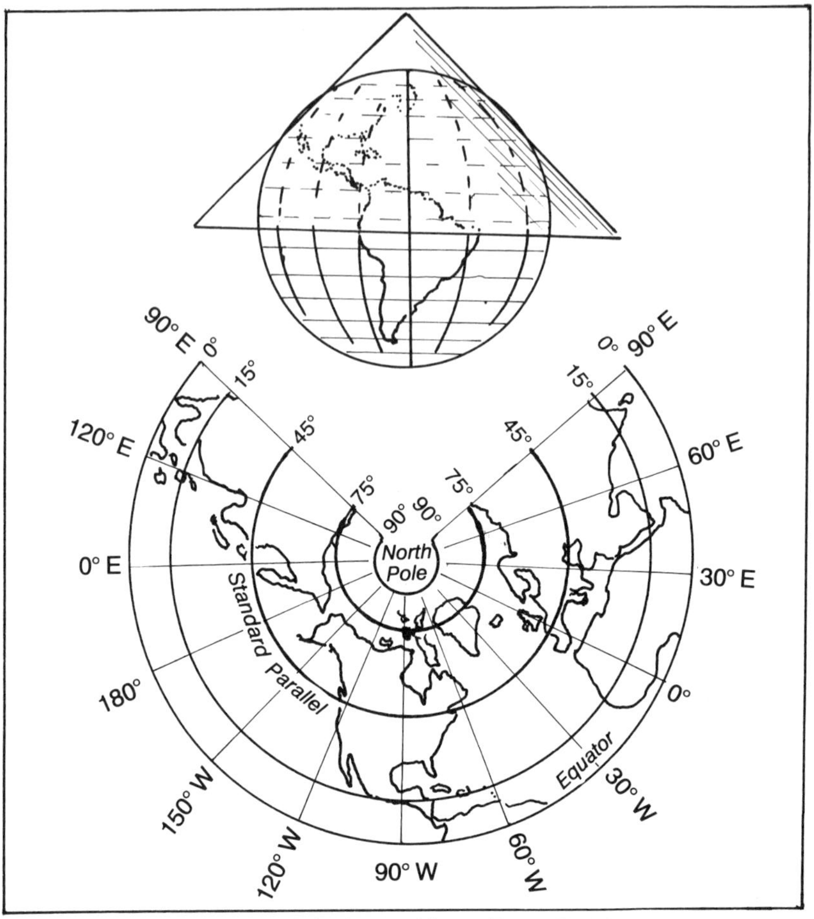

Figure 16 (adapted from Bowditch)

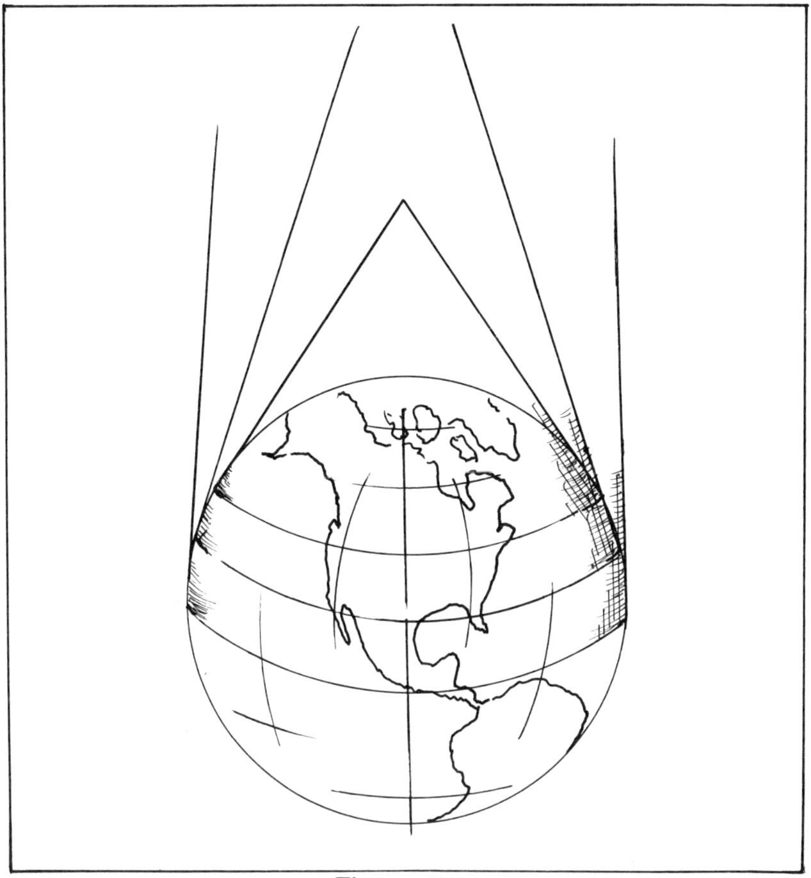

Figure 17

surface, we have a gnomonic projection (Fig. 18). Over large areas this will appear considerably distorted, but, as the projection of all points on the chart are from the center of the globe against an already flat surface, any straight line on the chart will be a great circle. These charts are referred to as great circle charts. In normal practice the mariner will draft his straight line between two points of his course and then take the latitude

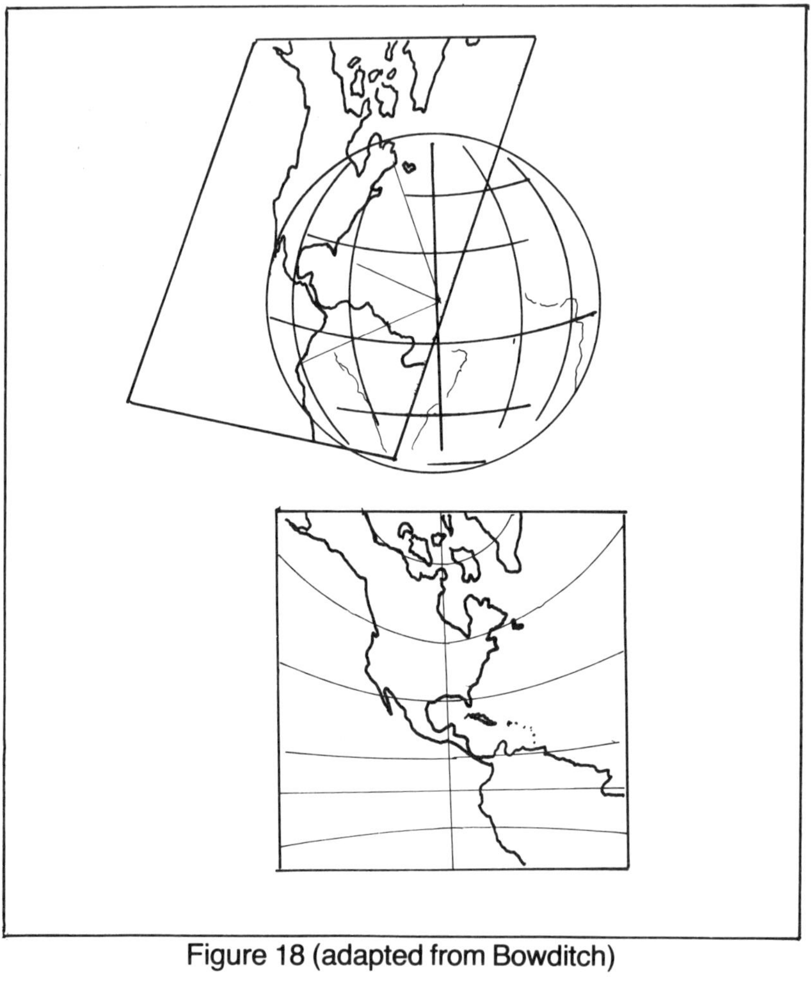

Figure 18 (adapted from Bowditch)

and longitude off at convenient points along the course and transfer these to his Mercator chart. In the example with this figure the single point of tangency is at 30° north latitude, 90° west longitude. If the point of tangency were at the equator, the meridians would appear vertical and parallel.

40. PILOT CHARTS

These charts are not intended for use in navigation, but in planning passages. A complete discussion of these aids to navigation is included in article 56.

41. CHART SOURCES

I hesitate to direct you to a source for government charts as such sources have changed their names several times over the past number of years. At some risk, however, I suggest writing to the Defense Mapping Agency Hydrographic Center (DMAHC) or the National Oceanic and Atmospheric Administration, National Ocean Survey.

There will be a merchant somewhere in your sailing area who sells navigational documents, and he will help you select those you need for the voyage you plan. Some may have to come from foreign sources, but he should know how to get them for you.

7

CHART NO. 1

A PAMPHLET of some thirty odd pages entitled *Chart No. 1 United States of America Nautical Charts and Symbols and Abbreviations* is inexpensive and available from the Defense Mapping Agency, Washington D.C., 20390 and from your local marine merchant. Your navigational charts will be covered with information in the form of illustrations, abbreviations, and symbols. Therefore, this pamphlet is a must for the new sailor. You'll be surprised at how many "old" sailors don't know about it.

I will not duplicate Chart No. 1. I will assume, however, that you will procure it before going further, and I will refer to it with that assumption in mind.

The purpose of this chart is to aid you, the navigator, in learning how certain helpful information will appear on your chart. There are other things you need to know about a good many of these bits of information, and I will cover these under separate subheads as follows:

42. COASTLINE (NATURAL FEATURES)

Under this subhead Chart No. 1 shows how these natural features will appear. You also need to know that your large scale chart will normally indicate the shoreline as it appears at some mean tide height. Where there is a wide range in tide, and a shallow bottom offshore, this can be important. Read the notes on your chart. Height and depth base data will be there somewhere. The section on natural features will be followed by several pages indicating how man-made features will appear on your chart.

43. LIGHTS

This is a particularly important section. Chart No. 1 is quite complete on the subject, but there is still a lot to learn that will be helpful.

Let's start with light characteristics. To find your position in the dark by the lights used as navigational aids, the lights must be identifiable and distinct from all other lights which will show in making a night landfall. This is accomplished by giving lights certain sequences of light and dark periods, or by color, or both. The colors used with U.S. lights are red (symbol R), green (symbol G), white (symbol W), and occasionally amber (symbol Am). If no symbol is used on the chart the light will be white.

The sequence of light and dark periods and the symbol for the various light characteristics is as follows:

Fixed—F This is a steady continuous light.

Fixed and Flashing—F Fl This is a fixed light that is varied at intervals with a flash of brighter intensity. The time period of the flash will be given with the identification of the light.

Fixed and Group Flashing—F Gp Fl This is again a fixed light with groups of two or more flashes at regular intervals.

Single Flashing—Fl This is a light that flashes once at regular timed intervals. The period of darkness always exceeds the period of light. The light flashes at a rate of not over thirty flashes a minute.

Group Flashing—Gp Fl This a group of two or more flashes followed by a period of darkness at regular intervals.

Continuous Quick Flashing—Qk Fl A quick flash is a flash that occurs at a rate of more than sixty flashes per minute. It is normally used as a warning of some kind.

Interrupted Quick Flashing—I Qk Fl This shows quick flashes for a period of approximately four seconds followed by a period of darkness of approximately the same time.

Short-Long Flashing—S-L Fl This is a short flash of about four-tenths of a second followed by a long flash of about four times that length. This is the Morse code "A" and it may be shown on your chart by the symbol, Mo(A).

Occultation—Occ This light is totally eclipsed at regular intervals with the period of light greater than the period of darkness.

Group-Occulting—Gp Occ This is occulting with two or more periods of darkness at regular intervals.

Equal Interval—E Int This is a light with equal intervals of light and darkness.

Along with light characteristics the identification of a light on your chart will include other helpful information. The larger the scale of the chart, the more information it will carry. Let's look at an example. On your large scale chart of the island of Oahu, next to Diamond Head Lighthouse is this abbreviated information:

Gp Occ (2) 10 sec 147 ft 17M

Translated this tells you that the light is group occulting with two periods of darkness in the group; that the groups appear every 10 seconds, that the light is 147 feet above mean high water, and that it should be visible for 17 miles. Let's take a look at that 17 miles.

44. RANGE OF VISIBILITY

You will remember that since the earth is round like a ball, or approximately so, you can only see a certain distance across the ocean because the surface falls away out of sight behind the horizon. The distance you can see depends on the height of your eye above the surface of the ocean and upon the height of the object. The distance that you can see a light at night will also depend upon the brightness of the light. In determining the range of visibility of a light, cartographers take both of these limiting factors into account. The height of Diamond Head Lighthouse, or any other lighthouse for that matter, is fixed. Therefore, the distance it can be seen from the horizon may be determined by considering the curvature of the earth. The eye that is viewing the light might be at any appropriate height depending on the size of the boat or ship. To be consistent the cartographer considers first the height of the object and then assumes a standard height for the eye of the observer. The U.S. chart makers use a height of eye of 15 feet. If the eye is higher and the light is bright enough, it can be seen from a greater distance than indicated. If the eye is lower, it will be shorter (Fig. 19). Because of other problems that may be variable such as light refraction, the distance is rounded off to the nearest nautical mile. Table IV (in the Appendix) gives the distance to the horizon for heights from one foot to two hundred thousand feet. You will see how to compute the distance an object can be seen by using the table.

You are in a sailboat about thirty feet long and sitting in the cockpit. Your eye is about five feet above the water. You have cleared the Channel Islands and are approaching the Los Angeles area. Point Vincent should be about one point off the port bow. A check with the chart shows it identified as follows: Gp Fl (2) 20 sec 185 ft 20 M. A check with Table IV shows that for a height of 185 feet the distance to the horizon is approximately 15.6 miles. The cartographer added 4.4 miles for the 15 feet height of eye. You are only 5 feet up so you will add 2.6 miles to

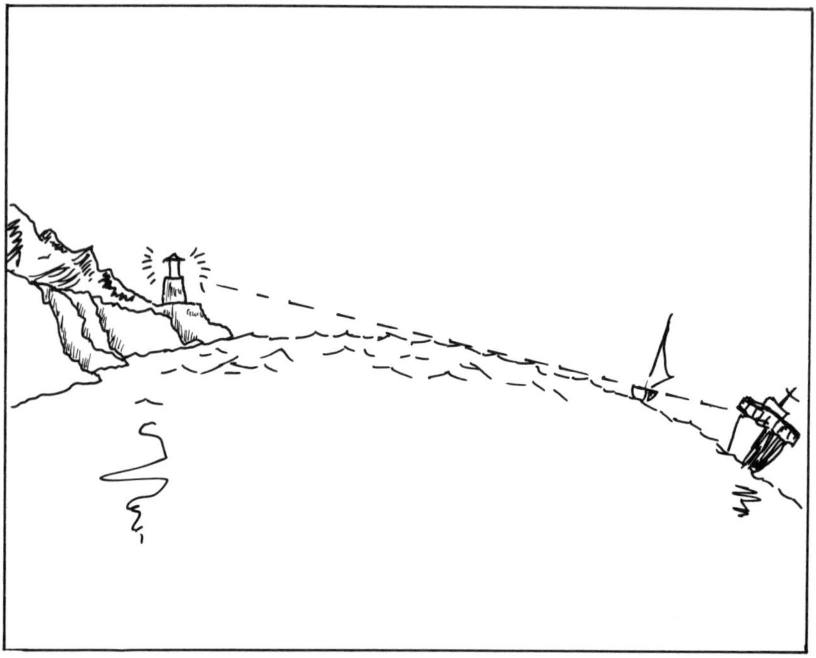

Figure 19

the 15.6 (from the table). You should see the light, if the weather is conducive to good vision, from just over 18 miles away.

Let me make another point with this example. When I looked up the distance to the horizon for 185 feet and added 4.4 to it for an eye height of 15 feet, I determined that Point Vincent was bright, and that the cartographer was using geographic range and not the luminous range. This was obvious because the height of the light plus 4.4 equaled the range printed on the chart. Let's look at another example where luminous range is used.

Do you remember *Sea Breeze*, the boat in the opening narrative of this book, whose navigator was searching for Nakalele light so that he could find his way to the finish line off Lahaina? If he had checked more thoroughly he would have found that light identified thus:

Fl 2½ sec 141 ft 7M

The geographic range from Table IV would place visibility at 13.5 miles, plus 4.4 for 15 feet height of eye, or a total of almost 17 miles. This is obviously not a very bright light. On a dark night he might have seen it from over 7 miles as its range indicates, but he could have known that it was not bright. The point I want to make, though, is that range of visibility can be used to approximate distance from the light, but only if it is a geographic range.

45. BOBBING THE LIGHT

If the sea is rough and the boat is small, the light will appear at its maximum range, just above the horizon, when the boat is high on a wave, and it will disappear when the boat is in the trough. You should not attempt to time the characteristics of the light at this point as it is impossible to get a complete sequence. Wait until it is clear above the horizon and then time the flashes or occlusions for identification. When the ocean is reasonably smooth, it is sometimes helpful, when near maximum range, to "bob the light" to determine its distance away. To do this the observer changes his height of eye by several feet.

If the light disappears as the height is lowered and re-appears when it is raised, a pretty good determination can be made as to the identity of the light. A good judgment of its distance can be made by considering the height at which it appears and disappears, and the height of the light. This is called bobbing the light.

46. SECTORS OF VISIBILITY

If you will examine your chart carefully, you will discover small dotted lines running obliquely away from the light in a good many cases. Follow the lines out a bit, and you will find a dashed line arcing toward shore which is labeled "Lt. obscured." This line is helpful in a number of ways. If you are well within the visible range of the light and visibility is good, but you still cannot see the light, you may be within the obscured sector where the light is hidden behind an outcropping of land or some other obstruction. If you then head seaward and the light suddenly appears, you will have an excellent line of position. You will know that you have just crossed that dotted line somewhere. I use such a line habitually when heading eastward from Diamond Head. Makapuu light is nine miles northeast of Diamond Head. It is obscured for some eight miles on my easterly course and then it pops into view. It is high and bright. It is easy to identify. I time my departure from Diamond Head and then time the moment Makapuu comes into view and have an excellent check on my speed for those first miles. I can also use this as one line of position (Chapter IX) for crossing with another to determine exact position.

47. COLOR SECTORS

Lights sometimes have different color sectors to convey special information. Let's go back to Diamond Head again. Westward from the lighthouse there are two dotted lines delineating two sectors. The area between the offshore line and the inshore is labeled "Red sector." Inside the inshore line is labeled "Light obscured." Here is some of the special information the pilot can gain from these two dotted lines. First, the south edge of the red sector (offshore edge) marks the line where inland rules of the road begin to apply when coming from seaward. Next, the red sector itself warns of nearness to shore and advises extra caution. The border between red and obscured leads directly to the outer marker for Honolulu harbor. Small boat sailors can also use this line for a night approach to Ala Wai harbor, as it crosses the range lights here just a hundred feet outside the flashing red lighted buoy marking the entrance.

Examine your chart before you start a voyage and locate these ready-made lines of position. They can be very helpful.

48. RANGE, OR LEADING LIGHTS

Range lights (sometimes called leading lights) are a pair of lights of distinctive color (from background lights) arranged to line up with a safe channel or other confined waterway. The light further away upon entering the channel is the higher of the two. The lights are shielded to show only over a narrow lateral range. When following the range the mariner keeps the two lined up so that the further one is directly over the nearer one. This assures him that he is in the center of the channel. If the upper light drifts to the right of the lower one he has moved to the right of center, if it moves left, he has drifted left. In many lengthy waterways with turns, there are a series of ranges with specific points indicated for changing from one to the next. When using any range it is necessary to determine when it is time to turn off. Range lights are located on dry land or fixed structures, and it is obvious that one must not follow a range ashore, to an unplanned landing.

49. CHANNEL LIGHTS

Here again, the details in Chart No. 1 are quite complete, but for emphasis once more I will repeat, "red right returning." In all United States harbors the markers on the right when entering will be red. Those on the left will be black. When lighted, either may be white, but if they are colored those on the right will be red, those on the left will be green.

This is not true with all nations. Before entering foreign waters find out what the system is.

50. LATERAL BUOY, BEACON SYSTEM

Everywhere in the world one of two basic systems of indicating the direction toward a danger is used. This is the purpose such markers perform. In the United States we use what is called the lateral system. In this system the numbering, color, shape, and lighting of the marker indicates the direction of the danger in relation to the course of the vessel. The system is applied assuming that the vessel is approaching land from seaward. When traveling along a coast, a different assumption needs to be made. For this purpose, a clockwise direction around the United States is assumed to be from seaward. In keeping with this assumption, where a series of buoys are placed along a shore to warn of a series of dangers, they will be red, and if numbered, will be numbered from north to south down the east coast, from east to west along the south coast, and from south to north up the west coast.

51. CARDINAL SYSTEM

Some maritime countries use the cardinal system with which the danger is on a particular bearing from the buoy or beacon. The direction depends on the characteristics, color, or shape of the buoy or beacon. Bearings are the cardinal directions, thus the name of the system.

Again, when planning a trip to foreign waters, it is essential that you obtain information on the system used. Most maritime nations have documents comparable to our Chart No. 1. These can be obtained from your document dealer, or he can find them for you.

52. RADIO AND RADAR STATIONS

Chart No. 1 will show you how to identify radio stations suitable for navigation, on your chart. It will illustrate how different types of stations are depicted and how their code identifiers can be found. The use of radio direction finders (RDF) is more appropriately discussed later in this text in Chapter X.

53. FOG SIGNALS

A fog signal is a signal in sound designed to warn the mariner of danger. As an examination of Chart No. 1 will show they are usually indicated on your chart by the name of the device producing the sound, or the type of sound, such as horn, whistle, bell, etc. Sound signals may be on buoys, beacons, or ships. There still remain at this writing sound systems actuated by the action of the sea. These devices are being replaced by mechanical devices capable of producing sound in specific patterns, much like lights do. The Light List, referred to in article 59 will provide information on fog signals in your area.

54. SOUNDINGS

Chart No. 1 will give you the information you need to interpret water depth data on your chart. You do need to know that United States charts give information in fathoms (six feet equals one fathom). Foreign nations may use some other measure. Table V gives the measure used by most nations, and its equivalent in feet.

55. DAY BEACON SHAPES AND COLORS

The last section in Chart No. 1 is devoted to several pages of color illustrations of day markers used in the United States. This section covers the four areas where there are differences, namely, in navigable waters, intercoastal waterways, western rivers and in states where the uniform marking system is used.

8

OTHER NAVIGATIONAL PUBLICATIONS

THESE ARE PUBLICATIONS that are not intended for use in daily navigation chores, but for planning and being prepared to meet sea and weather conditions.

56. PILOT CHARTS

Pilot charts are available for some oceans for every month of the year, for others, on a quarterly basis. They present in graphic form, and with adequate explanation, information gathered over the years to assist the sailor in planning his voyage. Let's take a good look at this information.

Average wind conditions for the time period of the chart are portrayed symbolically in each five degree square (Fig. 20). The symbol conveys a lot of information. The number in the circle indicates the number of days in one hundred that the wind is calm or light and variable. The arrows running to the circle represent first, the direction of the wind. The length of the arrow indicates the percentage of time the wind blows from the direction indicated. The length of all arrows combined represents 100%. When the line would be too long, a number is in a break in the arrow giving percentage of time. The feathers on the end of the arrow show the average velocity of the wind. Four feathers represents an average velocity of force four on the Beaufort scale (Table VI).

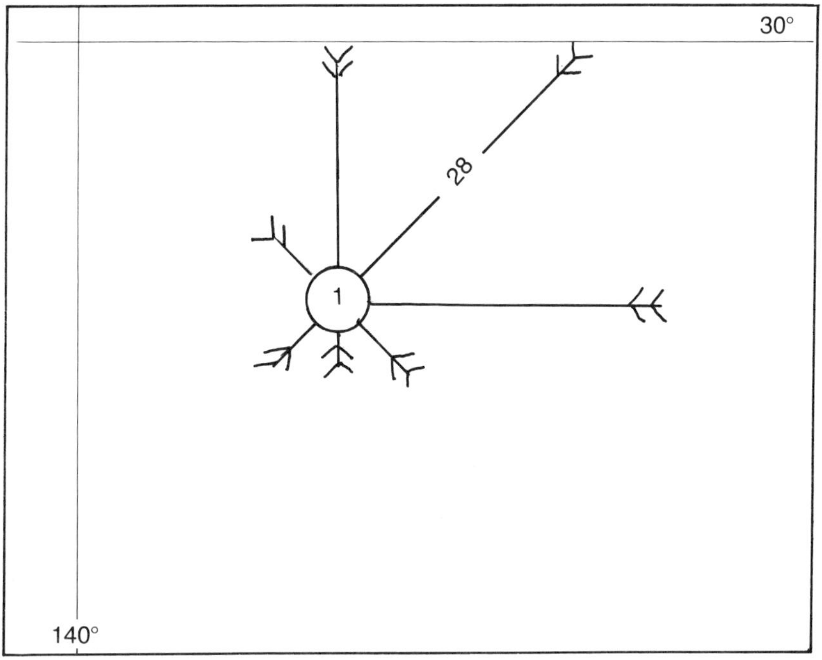

Figure 20

Elsewhere on your pilot chart will be information concerning average number of days when winds are of gale force or higher, when visibility is two miles or less, and what the average barometric pressure is. There is average sea and air temperature data, extent of floating ice in the ocean, and a history of violent storms in the area over the past few years. Magnetic variation is shown along with expected annual change. Prominent on the chart are large green arrows indicating prevailing currents. Where knowledge exists, the speed of the current is indicated. Major shipping routes are plotted.

57. THE COAST PILOT

The Coast Pilot editions are sometimes referred to as "The Sailings" or "Sailing Directions." In the United States they consist of a series of books, each book for a certain coastline. They are descriptive of the coastline, of prominent objects onshore or offshore, and of aids to navigation. They include data on service facilities, on how to navigate difficult passages and other information not suitable for reproduction on a chart.

U.S. Coast Pilots include data for navigable rivers, inland waterways, and for the coast of Canada. They are updated by supplement annually and are reprinted periodically.

58. TIDE TABLES AND LIGHT LISTS

Tide Tables are published annually by the National Oceanic and Atmospheric Administration and Light Lists by the Coast Guard. The tide tables are the tabulated times and extent of tide changes at various stations around the country and provide means of determining the particular tidal conditions between stations.

The Light Lists are published in a number of volumes covering the various coasts and inland waterways. These lists give detailed information on light characteristics, radio beacons, and fog signals. Changes are published periodically and also noted in the *Notice to Mariners*.

59. NOTICE TO MARINERS

This document is published weekly by the Defense Mapping Agency Hydrographic Center. It is designed to keep other documents constantly up to date. It indicates changes that should be made on your chart, and when new or revised charts will be printed. It warns of temporarily missing or moved aids to navigation. It warns of new or temporary dangers, special ocean activities such as yacht races, and other phenomena of interest to safety at sea. The *Notice to Mariners* should be available for consultation at the office of your regular marine document dealer. It can be obtained where the need exists, free of charge, through your local Coast Guard office.

This document is consulted all too infrequently, if at all. During a recent race from the mainland to Honolulu, a number of boats took a wrong turn as they approached the finish because they couldn't find a particular radio beacon on the dial. A check with the Coast Guard provided the information that the beacon had been discontinued for almost a year before this race. This information would have been in the *Notice to Mariners* the week following its removal.

9

LINE OF POSITION (LOP)

IN CELESTIAL NAVIGATION we construct a line of position by working out distance from, and direction to the geographical position of a celestial body. The geographical position is the point on the surface of the earth directly under the celestial body. In piloting, an art we might call terrestial navigation, we use objects on earth for the same purpose. A line of position, defined as a line on which we are located at some point, can only be as good as our instruments and our skill in using them can make it. Therefore, keep your instruments accurate and your skills up to date. There are a number of ways to develop a line of position. The following articles discuss the more important of these techniques.

60. BEARINGS

If we can determine the direction from our boat to a terrestial object which we can identify and locate on the chart we can then construct a line on the chart in the opposite direction from the object to us. To do this we simply add, or subtract 180° to, or from, the direction the object is from the boat. This will give an opposite or reciprocal bearing. We can be certain, within the accuracy of our determination, that we are somewhere on that line. With a single line of position we cannot be certain of our position but only that we are on the line.

61. PELORUS

The instrument normally used for taking bearings is called a pelorus, presumably named after a pilot who served under Hannibal. To the small boat sailor a pelorus is usually a simple, hand held compass with a sighting arrangement so constructed that the user can accurately sight a distant object and at the same time read the bearing in degrees from the compass. The hand held compass is subject to the same deviation problems the steering compass is. Therefore, you must take sights from a position away from local sources of interference.

If such a compass is not available, the boat can be used by heading it toward the object and reading the main compass. Remember, however, deviation must be considered and correction made from compass to magnetic, and then to true if you are using true bearings.

62. RANGES

When near land you can frequently find a number of incidental ranges in the natural or artificial structures which can be used to create lines of position. A range, as with range lights (art. 48), is the alignment of two objects which can be extended to create a line of position. For example, a radio tower and a church steeple, both of which can be identified and located on the chart, may form a line that can be extended seaward and thus form an ideal range. When the two objects come into line, the observer can be sure that he is somewhere on the extended line.

63. SECTOR LIMITS

Sector limits, discussed in article 46, form excellent ranges. When you pass from one sector to another, you know at the moment of passing, that you are on the sector limit line.

64. CIRCLE OF POSITION

If you are able to determine your distance from an object you can create a line of position by drafting a segment of a circle with a drafting compass, the measured distance from the object in the approximate direction you are from the object. There are a number of relatively inexpensive range finders on the market that can be used for determining distance. Radar, of course, if you are blessed with it, will serve this purpose admirably. Commercial vessels properly instrumented will have a number of techniques for measuring distance. Most of these, however, are not available to the average yachtsman.

65. FIX

As noted, a single line of position will not show exactly where you are. If two lines are obtained however, at approximately the same time, you have a fix. If you have two lines and know that you are on each, you can only be at the point where they cross. Ideally, when crossing the two bearings, the objects should be 90°, giving you a 90° cross. Two bearings taken from objects too close together will give lines of position crossing at an acute angle. In this situation a small error in bearings can cause a serious error in fix.

Navigators will frequently cross at least three lines spaced apart as much as possible, particularly when an accurate fix is desired. When plotting three lines they may not cross at exactly the same point but leave a small triangle at the point of intersection. This is caused by a number of things. It may result from an error in sighting; it may result because of the distance traveled between the sights; or it may be an error in drafting. Care can eliminate, or reduce these cases to a minimum. If the error results from the movement of the boat between bearings, this is something that can be corrected, and will be discussed later. When there is a small triangle, it is normal to assume that you are within the triangle. The safest assumption is that you are in the part of the triangle closest to any danger that may be near.

Any of the various lines of position, or combinations of the different kinds, can be used for obtaining a fix (Fig. 21). You may sight an object at the time of crossing the line of demarcation between sectors of a light; you may find two natural ranges at, or near, the same time; or you may cross a circle of position with a bearing line from the same object and get your fix.

Now take a good look at Figure 21 to get practice working out fixes. In this example I will use a frequently made voyage for sailors in the Hawaiian Islands where I live. It is from Honolulu on the island of Oahu to Lahaina, Maui. I use this area, not just because it is in home waters, but also because it makes a fine practice course for piloting problems. Let me say, in this instance, that I am sailing a thirty foot sloop to Lahaina for a long weekend. If the trade wind is normal it will be blowing from the east-northeast at about fifteen knots. From experience, I know that it will be dead on the nose from the east shortly after I have Molokai abeam. I therefore sail well above my course until I reach the wind shift, and then fall off to sail around the south point of Lanai. You will note the base course of 111° magnetic. I choose the south point of Lanai to avoid beating through the rough water in the channel between Molokai and Lanai.

The wind, which is normally strong during the day, usually drops in the evening, as does the sea, so I start after sundown. I check the time as I harden up sails and take my departure from Diamond Head. Once I am on the wind I check my compass. I am holding at 100° magnetic. This is 11° above my course, and it should put me in a good position for the wind shift I will meet as I near Molokai.

My knotmeter reads just over five knots, and I can see by studying the chart that the dotted line marking the obscured sector of Makapuu light is about eight miles out. Shortly before one and a half hours have passed I get out my hand bearing compass and make ready to take a bearing from Diamond Head as Makapuu comes into view. I watch. Makapuu appears. I read

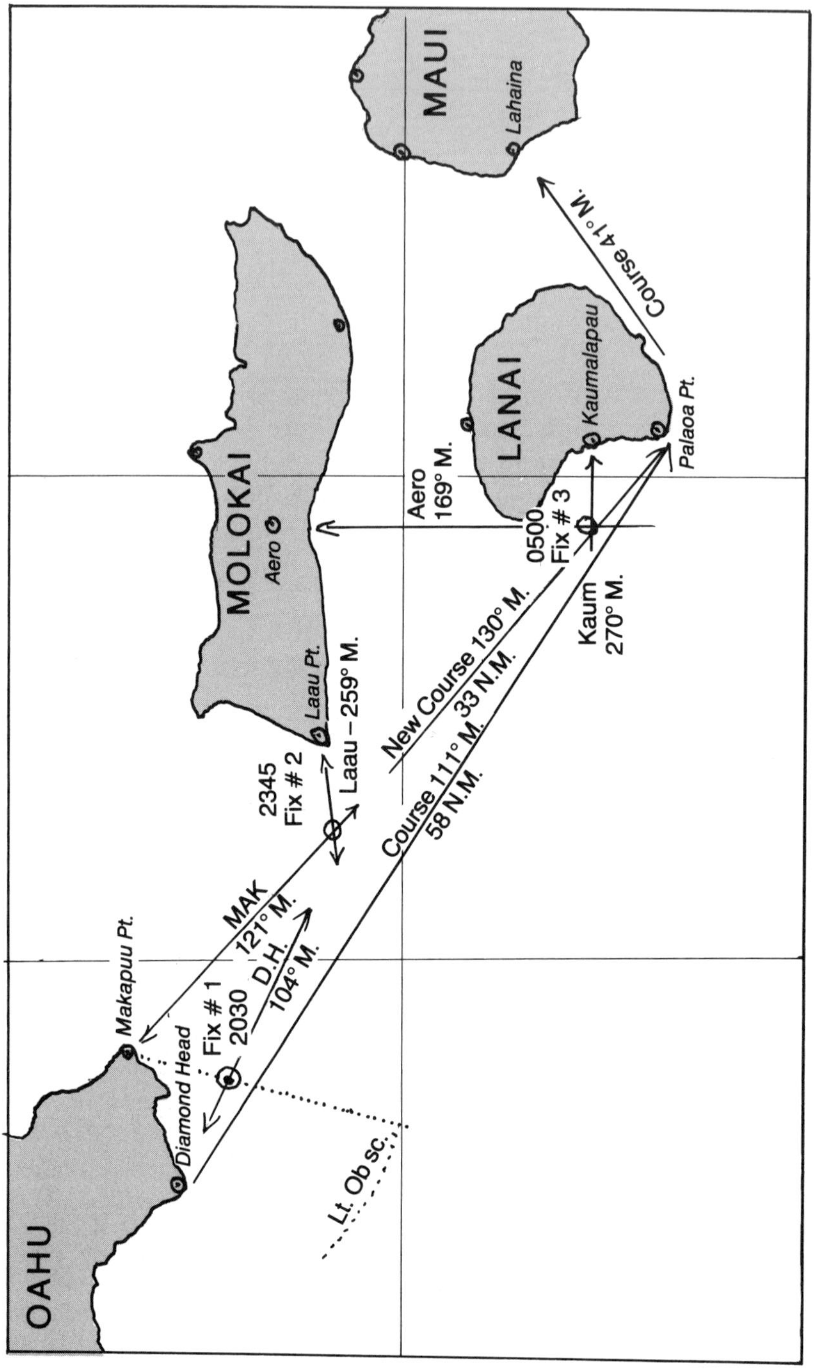

OAHU
Diamond Head
Makapuu Pt.
Fix # 1
2030
D.H.
104° M.
MAK
121° M.
Lt. Ob sc.
2345
Fix # 2
Laau – 259° M.
Laau Pt.
MOLOKAI
Aero
Course 111° M.
58 N.M.
New Course 130° M.
33 N.M.
Aero
169° M.
0500
Fix # 3
Kaum
270° M.
LANAI
Kaumalapau
Palaoa Pt.
Course 41° M.
MAUI
Lahaina

Figure 21

the bearing to Diamond Head at 284°. I then subtract 180° from that and get a reciprocal bearing of 104°, and with either my protractor or parallel rule, I measure and draft that bearing out from Diamond Head to where it crosses the dotted line from Makapuu. I have my first fix. I can learn a couple of other things from this work. First, by timing the moment Makapuu appeared, and comparing it with the time Diamond Head was abeam, I can check my speed through the water. Second, my heading from Diamond Head was 100°, but now I bear 104° from Diamond Head. I am making 4° of leeway (art. 81).

I continue on my way and in about another hour and fifteen minutes Diamond Head light falls below the horizon. Visibility from my height of eye is about fifteen miles, and so I divide the distance by the time and conclude that I am moving along about as planned.

I sail on, holding my heading around 100° and finally, four and a half hours out, I spot a light off the port bow. It appears to be flashing irregularly. Therefore, I wait to time the flashes until I am sure that it is clear of the horizon and not hidden at times by waves. When it is clear, I time it at two and one half seconds. This identifies it as Laau Point light. Makapuu is still there off the port quarter. I take a bearing from it and read my compass at 301°. Then I take a bearing from Laau and read 79°. I go below to my chart where I subtract 180° from the Makapuu reading and add 180° to the Laau reading, plot the bearing lines, and cross them for my second fix.

Back on deck I soon notice that the wind has become light and variable. This is expected, we are in the lee of west Molokai, and soon the wind will be back and coming down the channel heading us. And then it does. We fall off to a new heading of 130° magnetic, and the sails fill. I plot this course on the chart and find that it will bring me safely to Palaoa Point, Lanai, right where I want to be. We settle down for a romp across the channel between Molokai and Lanai. Laau Point and Makapuu lights soon disappear below the horizon astern. The lights ahead on Lanai aren't very bright. I won't see them until I am within six or seven miles. The night is dark. All I have for a reference point now is that aero beacon high on the slopes of Molokai. I hold 130° on the compass carefully, because that western point of Lanai is dark, and I could run onto it if I sailed too high on the wind. The wind gradually moves aft as we sail across the channel, so I ease sheets and make out like a bandit. The knotmeter is up to seven knots. Finally, the aero beacon is off the port quarter, and there to port ahead is Kamalapau. I take a quick bearing on both lights, change them to reciprocal bearings, and plot my position at fix number three. I am soon in the lee of Lanai sailing in smooth water, and I see the first traces of dawn reaching up over Lanai. It's a daylight trip from here on, and I can see my destination nestled in the green of sugar cane against the steep slopes of west Maui.

66. THE RUNNING FIX

Frequently in pilot waters, amateurs will want to, and should, keep a reasonably accurate account of their location. This is particularly true if the waters are unfamiliar, or if there is a chance of diminishing visibility. A good pilot will always remain aware of his position and be prepared for any eventuality which may occur.

At times it is necessary to maintain a running fix by crossing lines of position taken at different times and adjusting them to a common time. We could have used just such a fix on that leg of the trip from Laau Point to the lee of Lanai (Fig. 22).

Let's go back and sail that leg again and see how we might keep a fix with only one light in view. You will remember, we could see and identify on the chart, the aero beacon on Molokai. You will also note on the illustration that we kept a record of the time of each fix. In this illustration we will start with number two fix at 2345. The bearing line from Laau Point is labeled A. For the next two hours we are close hauled in light to moderate air, and our knotmeter shows five knots. We checked it against the time of our fixes (see Table VII) and are satisfied that it is correct. An accurate determination of speed is necessary with this problem. At 0145 I have moved along my course a

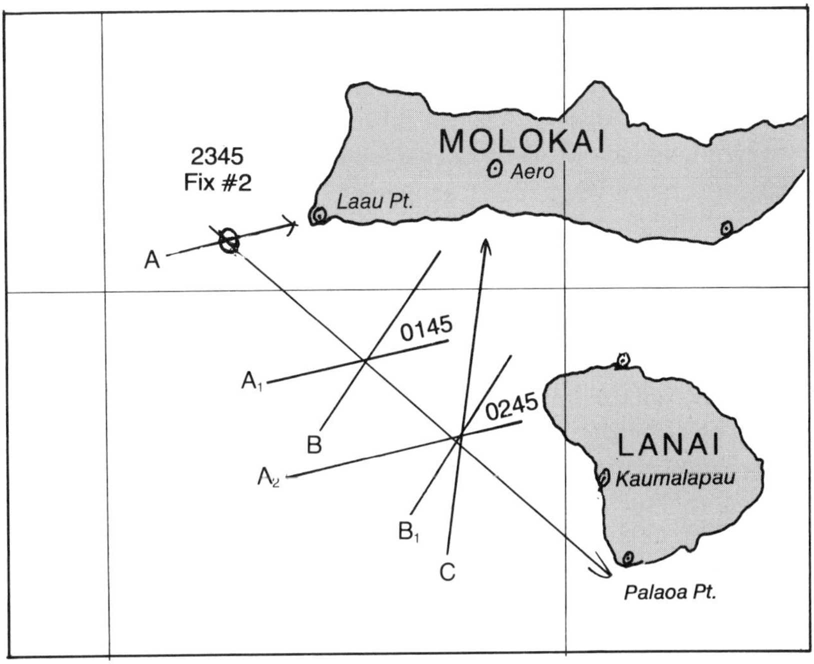
2345
Fix #2
MOLOKAI
Aero
Laau Pt.
A
0145
A1
B
0245
LANAI
A2
Kaumalapau
B1
C
Palaoa Pt.

Figure 22

distance of ten miles. I now take my parallel rule and advance line A ten miles along the course keeping it at the same angle. The advanced line is labeled A_1. Next, I take a bearing on the aero beacon, subtract 180° and find that I bear 203° from it. I plot this and label it B. Where it crosses line A_1 is where we are if my determination of distance over the bottom is correct.

At this point let's say our speed picks up to seven knots as we ease sheets and begin reaching. One hour later at 0245 I again advance line A to A_2 and line B to B_1 in the same manner as the first advance of line A. Now I take another bearing from the aero beacon and plot it as line C. Again, if my judgment of distance over the bottom is accurate, I have a good fix with just one light showing. While making assumptions, let's go back to Laau Point and make a new one. Let's assume that rather than a bearing from the point I used a range finder and got a distance from it. With this information I drafted a circle of position (Fig. 23).

The first bit of information we get from studying this illustration is that with a range measurement, and a bearing from the same object, in this case Laau Point, we can obtain an excellent fix. The point at the moment, however, is advancing a circle of position. Line A in this illustration is the circle drafted five miles from Laau Point. This is the distance recorded by the range finder. To advance a circle of position, I must advance Laau Point light the distance run between fixes, and draft a new circle to be crossed with the bearing from the aero beacon, line B. The second advance is also shown, but note that the circle is now a very poor indicator. It is almost in line with bearing line C and thus gives no real indication of where we are on line C.

67. CURRENT EFFECT

The effect of current or leeway clearly can throw off a fix indicated by an advanced line of position. It is difficult to be aware of this unless we know the direction and speed of the current or leeway, and take it into account in advancing the

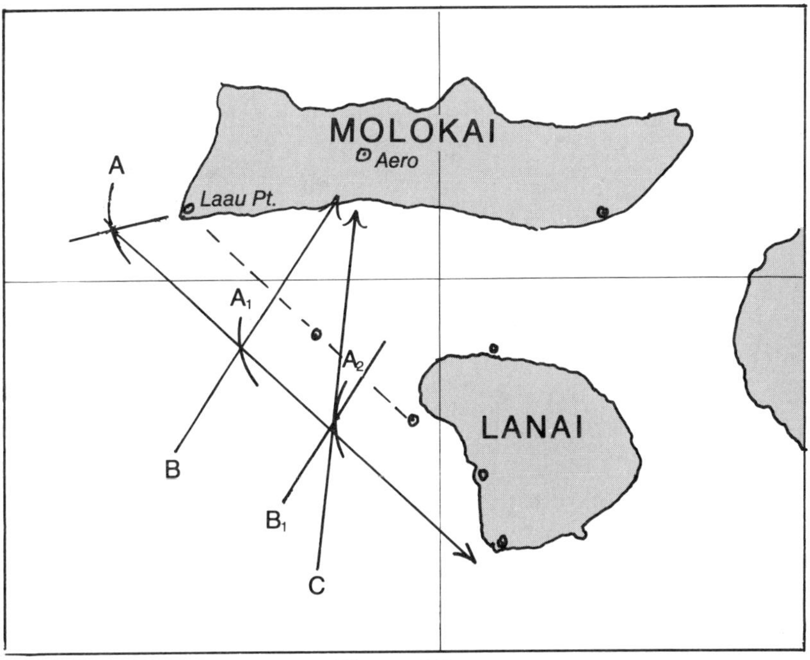

Figure 23

line. There are some things we can do about current, however, and I will discuss these shortly.

A direct head current, when advancing a line from a bearing taken abeam, will cause our track to appear further from the object sighted than it actually is. (Fig. 24) In this example we are sailing along a shore on course as indicated. With one lighthouse in view, we work out a bearing from it at line A. An hour later we believe that we have advanced along the course to line A_1. We advance line A to this position. Unknown is a strong head current and we are actually at the dashed line a. When we take our second bearing on the light and cross it with the erroneously advanced line, it crosses several miles further at sea than it would if the advance had been properly reflective of the current. This can be a dangerous situation, particularly if there are offshore dangers that must be avoided.

If the current in another situation is following, the effect will be the opposite (Fig. 25). As you can see in this illustration the indicated position will be inshore from the actual position.

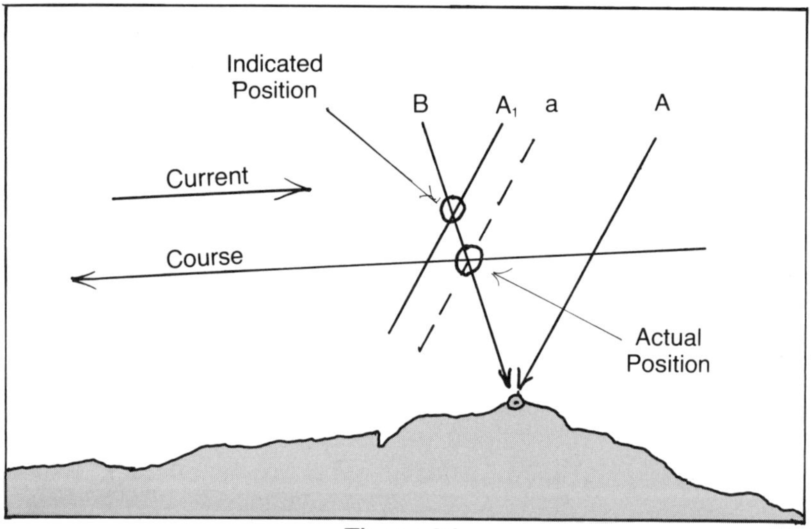

Figure 24

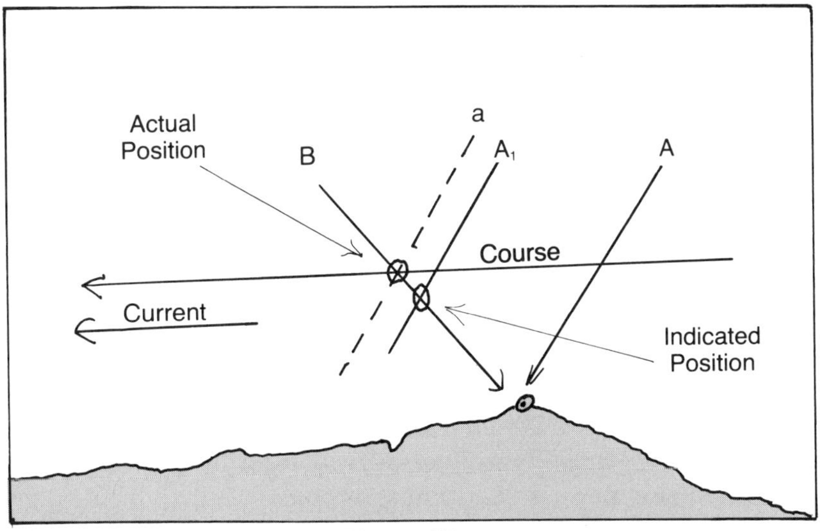

Figure 25

An unknown oblique current can be a teaser. It will not make its presence known with a first advance, but after a second advance, error will be apparent (Fig. 26). In this illustration our assumed course is indicated by the solid line. We have an oblique current running offshore from the port quarter. We obtain bearing line A, proceed to A_1 without knowledge of the current. The small dotted line a, shows where this line should be as in the previous example. At this first advance we do have an indication that we are to the right of course, but this indication is only partially correct. The dashed course made good line indicates where we actually are.

We sail on for another hour and take a third bearing on the lighthouse at line C. We advance A and B to cross with the new line and have three indicated positions forming a large triangle. We now know something is wrong.

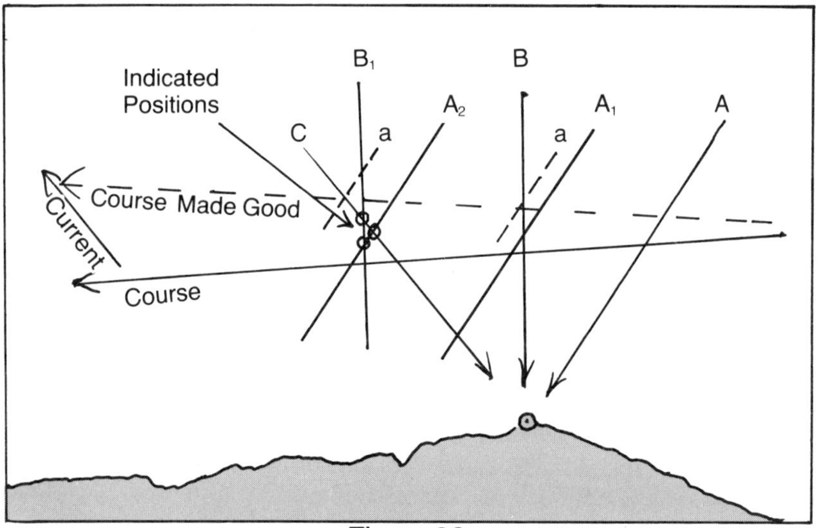

Figure 26

When this happens we can, if necessary, find out what our track has been, and see if our speed through the water and our heading have been consistent. To do this we take a small strip of paper and mark off our distance traveled through the water between bearing lines on the edge of the strip (Fig. 27).

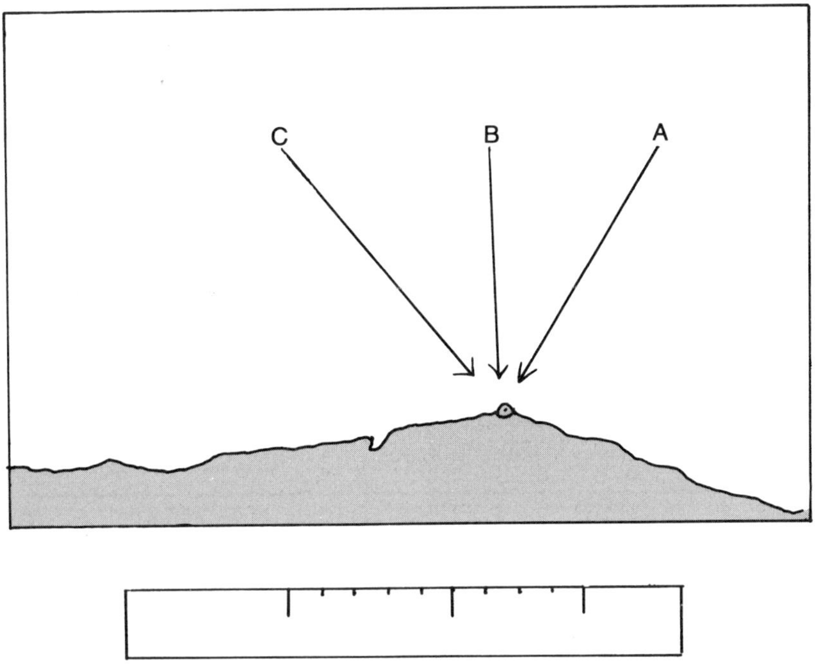

Figure 27

In this illustration, we traveled four miles between A and B and five miles between B and C. These distances are marked off to the scale of the chart we are using. Next, (Fig. 28) we fit the strip of paper with its indicators to the lines A, B, and C, on the chart. This is done by trial and error until we find where they fit. The dots on the strip will only fit on a line that is parallel to the course actually made good during the period that the bearing lines were taken.

If a reliable fix was made at some time not too long before erroneous running fixes were made, a fair estimate of the current can be made by extending a plot from the reliable fix in the direction of the course made good as shown by the strip of paper. The intersection of this plot with any of the bearing lines can be considered a reasonable fix. If a good DR is available for the same time period, then the speed and direction of the current can be accurately estimated. The direction of the current is from the DR to the fix. The speed is the length of the line between the two measured to the scale of the chart and divided by the time between the two positions (Fig. 29).

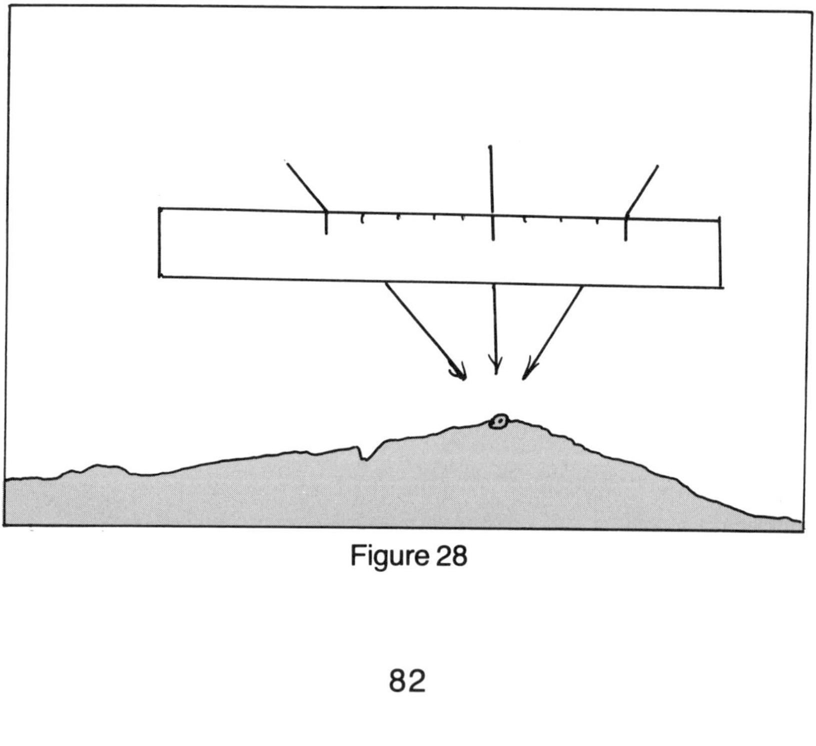

Figure 28

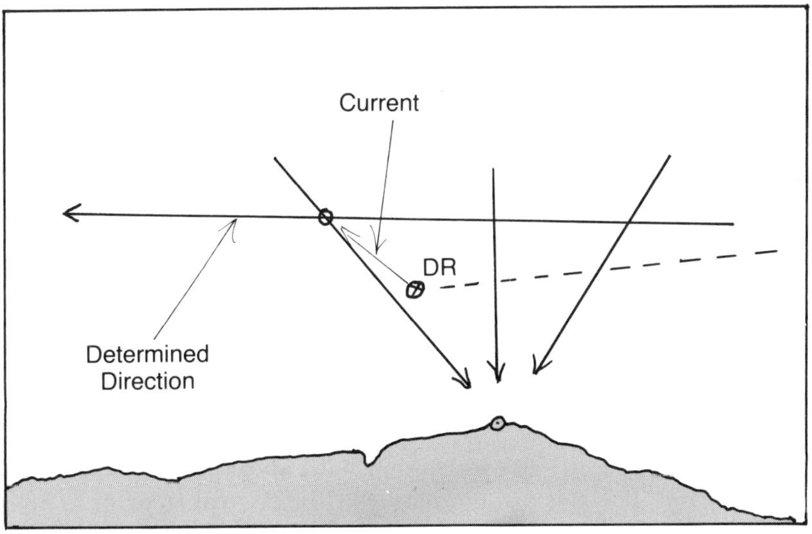

Figure 29

68. FIX WITHOUT PLOT

Your copy of Bowditch will have a table from which accurate positions can be determined by the change in bearings of an object as compared with course and distance run between bearings.

Most amateur pilots do not take the time and effort necessary to use these tables. We can, however, take the time to remember, or make a quick check in a manual such as this, to find some of the easier solutions.

For example: We are sailing along a coast and locate an object ahead such as a lighthouse. We take a bearing on the lighthouse when it is 45° off the bow. If we then note the time and the speed of our vessel and wait until the lighthouse is broad on the beam (90°), we will know that our distance from the lighthouse when it is abeam is exactly the same as the distance run between bearings. This is called "doubling the angle on the bow," or "bow and beam bearings."

There are a number of other bearing differences that are worth remembering, or knowing about, so that they can be looked up. If the first bearing is 63.5° and the second 90°, the distance off is about twice the distance run. If the angles are 71.5° and 90°, it is about three times the distance run.

Another technique is a simple time-speed formula. Measure the time in seconds it takes for a beam bearing to change 16°. Multiply this by speed in knots. Divide by 1,000. The answer is distance from the object in nautical miles at the time it was abeam.

69. BOTTOM PROFILE

A good many yachts are equipped with sounding instruments of some kind. It is not unusual for a sailboat racer to want to hug a coast in order to pick up on- and offshore breezes. During daylight hours bearings can be taken to determine distance offshore. At night along an unmarked section of coastline, the fathometer becomes the important instrument for maintaining distance. When using such a device you should be careful to examine the chart for off-lying dangers arising abruptly from the bottom and be careful to avoid them. In the fog near shore when other aids may be lost from view, your fathometer may help save the day, particularly when depths are relatively consistent, or when other bottom features such as ridges or trenches can be easily identified. When in doubt of your position under these conditions, it is good practice to make regular periodic checks of the depth along the track, such as every half-mile or so, record these on transparent paper to the scale of your chart for the distance run and then try to match them with the depths on your chart over the presumed course. You must remember that sounding data are normally made from mean low water, and, if the tide range is wide, you must allow for the condition of the tide at the time of the depth measurements. This technique is by no means precise, but in a pinch it can frequently be helpful in finding your position.

70. RELATIVE BEARINGS

We have been discussing bearings as angles from north, or as points of the compass. Bearings relative to the direction in which the vessel is headed are frequently used to indicate verbally the direction in which an object is located. These directions are less precise than those expressed in degrees but are useful because they are quickly communicable and thus helpful in relaying information concerning dangers to navigation (Fig. 30).

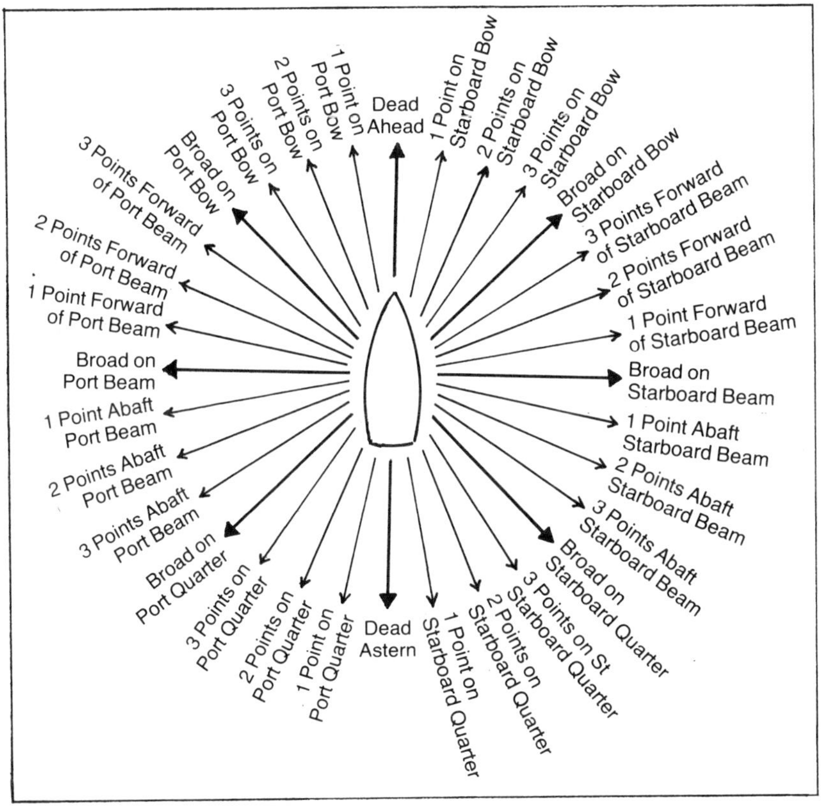

Figure 30

These relative bearings can be expressed even more generally by such expressions as "ahead, on the port bow, on the starboard quarter," and so forth. Approximate degrees either right or left of the heading may also be used at times to indicate relative bearings. These directions are useful for passing along information to the helmsman or master, but are not intended to be accurate enough for plotting position.

10

RADIO DIRECTION FINDER (RDF)

THE SUBJECT of electronic navigation is a subject unto itself and covers a wide range of electronic tools. Some of these tools are economically available to the amateur, some may not be. We will only discuss the RDF. An RDF can be purchased in a number of relatively inexpensive models, and a good many boats are equipped with one. If you are boating in an area where there are frequent periods of fog, an RDF is a *must.*

RDFs come in a variety of forms from the simplest hand held unit to the permanently mounted installation with an outside loop antenna and a visual readout. Your electronics merchant will help you select the model best suited to your boat and your pocketbook. Whatever RDF you select, it will perform the job in approximately the same way. The first key to mastering the instrument is to understand the working of the antenna. All antennas, called loops, are designed to stand on a vertical axis which allows them to rotate. At the base of the antenna and around the rotating axis is a compass rose with a pointer which will indicate the position of the antenna. When the antenna is broadside toward the radio station to which it is tuned, it will receive a maximum amount of energy from the station, and the volume of the signal will be high. When it is oriented edge on toward the station, the signal will be weakest (Fig. 31). This position is called the null, and is used to indicate

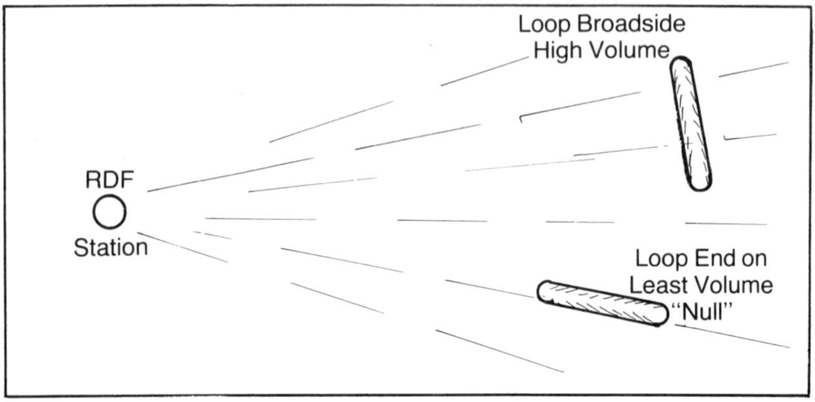

Figure 31

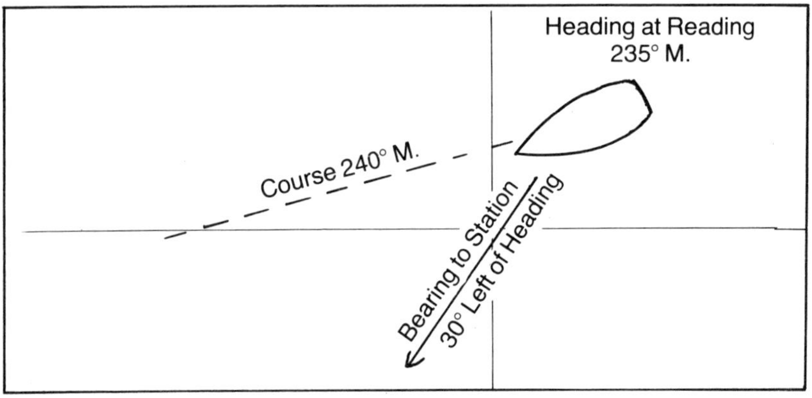

Figure 32

direction toward the station because it is easier to identify than the point where the volume is the highest.

If your RDF is other than the hand held model, it must be mounted so that the compass rose, called in this case an azimuth circle, is oriented with its zero point in line with the keel of your boat, in the same way that the compass is mounted with the lubber's line. Some RDFs will be provided with means for adjusting the azimuth circle so that it can be aligned with magnetic north and thus give a reading of magnetic direction. Those mounted in line with the keel give readings relative to the heading of the vessel. If this method is used, the boat must be held steady on course while readings are taken, or they will be wrong. I sail in rough waters where at times during a passage the helmsman is doing a good job if he keeps the compass from swinging less than 10° on each side of the heading desired. In these conditions I find a second method better. I mount a second compass near the RDF (but not so near as to effect the compass) and set the antenna close to the null. As the boat's heading swings, I watch the compass until the null appears and note the compass heading at that time. I then work out radio bearings relative to that compass heading. For example, let's say our desired course is 240°. We are in a following sea, and the boat is yawing at least 10° to either side (Fig. 32). I am tuned in to a station off the port bow. I will then rotate the antenna and listen, or, if I have visual readout, watch for the null to pass as the boat yaws. My antenna is set at 30° to the left of dead ahead. The null is within the yawing arc of the boat, so that I now watch the compass as the null passes. I may do this for several minutes until I am sure of where on my secondary compass the null appears. In this example my compass reads 235° at the null. The azimuth circle reads 30° left; I subtract 30° from 235°; and I have a magnetic bearing to the station of 205°.

Just as with a visual bearing, I can subtract 180° and find a reciprocal bearing from the station to me. This is my line of position by RDF. I can cross an RDF line with a second or third RDF line for a fix, or I can cross it with any other line I can work out.

71. RDF ERROR

I have already discussed the mounting of the RDF in line with the keel of the boat so that it will read true in relation to the heading. There are other problems with mounting as indicated in article 72.

72. QUADRANTAL ERROR

Just as the magnetic parts of your boat can cause compass error and deviation, so can they cause RDF error. This is called quadrantal error because it is normally greatest for directions broad on the bow and broad on the quarter. Your radio technician can help you solve this problem. However, you can swing the ship yourself to make checks on accuracy. Most RDFs have a sighting arrangement on the antenna. With this you can place the boat in a known position in sight of a known broadcasting antenna. You can tune for the null and then sight on the station. If you can't sight from the location of the RDF, you can use your pelorus and compare readings.

If your RDF is to be used for accurate navigation, see that it is mounted in a place where the error is least; and if you continue to record error, make a deviation card just as you do for your compass error.

73. COASTAL REFRACTION

Radio waves are refracted somewhat as they pass over a coast line at an oblique angle. Radio stations designed for RDF have accounted for this by placement of the transmitting antenna on, or near, the shore. These are your first and best stations for direction finding. Some aero radio stations show on your chart, and these are usually suitable second choices. Stations that are located well inland or in a valley will not be suitable, for their waves can be badly refracted by surrounding terrain. Normally these do not appear on the marine chart. Commercial radio stations with wave lengths of under 800 kHz can give fairly reliable bearings if their antennas are located near the shoreline. A word of caution, many radio stations have studios at one location with antennas at another location, perhaps miles away. You tune on the antenna, but unless you know where it is you can't judge the reliability of the station. Your radio technician may have a listing of suitable stations in your area.

74. POLARIZATION ERROR

Any radio bearings taken near sunrise or sunset should be suspect. There are likely to be changes taking place in the ionosphere which may alter the direction of movement of radio waves.

75. THE MERCATOR CHART PROBLEM

Radio waves travel the shortest distance from the station to your receiver, thus, they come by great circle (the curved line on your Mercator chart). Meridians are great circles as is the equator. With a radio station directly north or south of you, or directly east or west when you are on the equator, there will be no error when plotting a line of position from the station. As the circumstances of location deviate from these, the error when plotting on a Mercator chart will increase. This same error also increases with distance between the transmitter and receiver. It can also increase with latitude.

The RDF is a good tool for direction finding at distances of under two hundred miles. In this range and in mid-latitudes, error will be minimal and can be ignored. For longer ranges consult Bowditch. There are tables there along with instruction for using them in converting this error.

76. 180° AMBIGUITY

As noted, if the end of the loop antenna is pointing at the broadcasting antenna, this is the null, and volume will be at its lowest, no matter which end of the antenna is so pointed. If the general direction of the station is not known then a possible

180° error is in the making. Some of the better RDFs correct this problem with a design which indicates the proper end. Without this device, and when in doubt, other steps must be taken. A series of bearings taken over a period of time on the questionable station will soon remove the doubt. The time span necessary depends on the speed of the boat and the distance from the station. For example, if you tune in a station 40° off the starboard bow, or, 140° to port off the other end of the loop, and after awhile you wonder to which you have tuned, a few miles on the same course will soon tell. If the antenna is off the starboard bow, it will move back, and the right end of the antenna will move with it as it holds the null. If it is to port, the left end will move back. A station dead ahead or dead astern presents a problem in volume since that is all you have to differentiate between them. Volume should increase as you approach a station, and decrease as you sail away from it. Set your volume so that you can just hear it and wait for the change. Of course, if you get a cross bearing from another station you will have eliminated the problem.

77. RDF HOMING

One of the best and most historic uses of your RDF is to find your way home by tuning in the station at the harbor mouth and keeping it right on the flagstaff until you are home. The problem here is much like the problem when following a range. You have to know when to get off the track or you might run right up to the station on shore. It has happened. A cross bearing occasionally from another station is the easy way to know where you are as you approach. You can also turn aside with the station at 90° and get bow and beam bearings (art. 68) and work your way in from the distance determined by easy steps.

Homing away from a station, if we can call it homing, is another matter. Let's suppose we want to sail to a certain point that is 100° magnetic from a handy RDF station. We start out headed 100° with the RDF showing the station directly astern.

After an hour we find that we are still holding 100° but the station is now 10° to starboard from astern. We can conclude that we are in quite a cross current. The thing to do is to take a jog to starboard, come on course again, and see if it is back astern where it belongs. If it isn't, take another jog, or another until it is. You had best get below and figure out what the current is also, so that you can account for it in your heading. We'll get to that problem, allowing for current, next.

11

COMPENSATING FOR CURRENT

THE HORIZONTAL movement of water, for whatever reason caused, is called current. The direction it is moving is called set, and the speed at which it moves is called drift. Leeway is defined as the action of wind on a vessel causing it to move leeward. Both will have an effect on the direction and speed of a boat over the bottom as opposed to through the water. It is interesting to note that winds and currents are referred to differently. A north wind comes from the north. A north current goes toward the north.

Some currents such as tidal currents will change in both direction and speed as the tide changes. Major ocean currents are relatively constant over long periods of time. These currents can generally be counted on, although they may change in speed and direction somewhat because of changing wind patterns.

Your Coast Pilot will include an estimate of the well established currents along a coast. Pilot charts, as indicated earlier, will include ocean current information in graphic form for areas where sufficient observations have been made to make the information reliable. More precise information is available for a good many places in Tide and Current tables prepared by the U.S. Coast and Geodetic Survey. Ask about them at your chart merchant's store.

Professional sailors are likely to refer to all factors which cause error in dead reckoning as current, and thus, consider the difference between a DR position and a fix for the same time as a result of current. Sailboat sailors who know their boats well are likely to know what their leeway is for a given set of conditions. They will consider this when plotting a course and allow for it at the outset of a cruise. If set, drift, and leeway are known, or can be reasonably estimated, allowances can be made in planning a course. If not known, they can be ascertained from fix to fix.

78. HEAD AND FOLLOWING CURRENT

Very simply stated, if I am moving north at a speed of four knots in a current that is moving south at four knots, I will remain stationary in relation to the bottom. If I am moving north at ten knots in a south flowing current of two knots, my speed over the bottom will be eight knots. The speed of the current is simply subtracted from the speed of the boat through the water. The converse is true with a following current. If my boat speed is ten knots through the water in a following current of two knots, my speed over the bottom will be twelve knots. In this instance the current speed is added to obtain speed over the bottom. In either instance there is no effect on my track.

79. BEAM CURRENT

The speed-track effect is almost reversed with current from directly abeam (Fig. 33a). In this illustration we are planning a trip across a channel to a little bay twelve miles away. The course is 90° true, and in our power cruiser we will be traveling at eight knots. We are familiar with the channel and are aware of a current flowing south at two knots. This illustration shows what will happen if we ignore the current and hold to a heading of 90°. Starting at A we hope to be at B in one hour. The current, however, has carried us south two miles during that hour and we find ourselves at C. Notice that our speed over the bottom

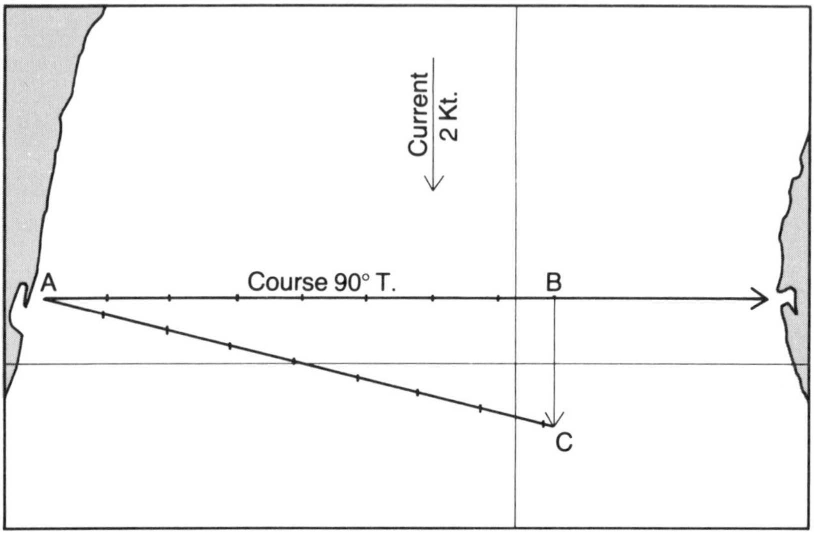

Figure 33a

has remained at close to eight knots, but not exactly. The hypotenuse of the triangle, A to C is slightly longer than the leg A - B. Our track, on the other hand, is about 14° off course.

Now, let's go back and plan for that current before we start (Fig. 33b). We know that we will be carried south two miles in one hour while going through the water eight miles. First we will plot those two miles south from our starting point at A, and call that position C. From C measure off the eight miles through the water that we will be making and extend a line this long to the point where it intersects course line at B. Next with our protractor, or a parallel rule, from the compass rose on the chart, we will measure the angle of the line from C to B. In this instance it is 76°. This is the heading we will have to hold from A to be at B, on course, after one hour. You can see by measuring line A-B that our speed over the bottom is slightly under eight knots. We are, however, on course and can expect to arrive at our destination without a change in heading.

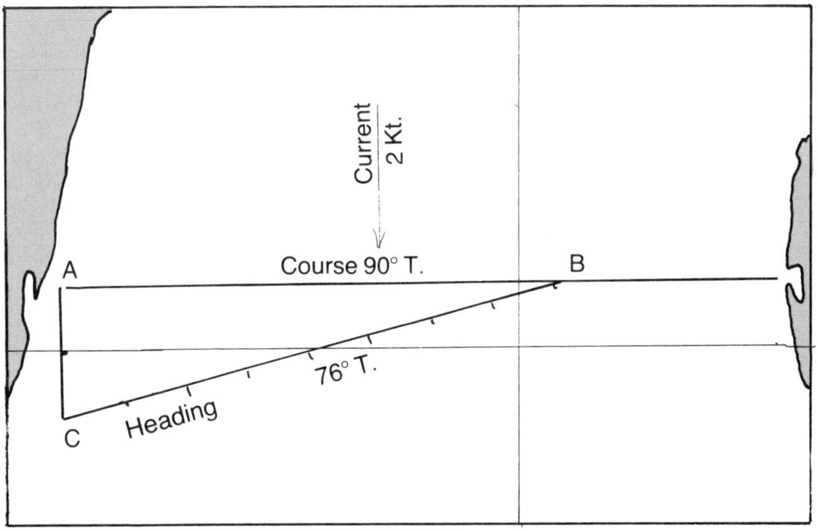

Figure 33b

80. OBLIQUE CURRENT

Now let's examine a situation in the same boat with a current that is at an oblique angle to our desired course (Fig. 34a). The course is still due east, 90° true. It is still a two-knot current, but this time it is flowing in the direction 140° true. In these conditions if we hold a heading of 90° starting at A and speed of eight knots through the water, we will end up after one hour at C, having traveled the distance at a speed over the bottom of 9.5 knots. We make our correction to maintain course for this situation just as we did with a beam current (Fig. 34b). We plot the flow of the two-knot current from A to C. From there we measure off the speed through the water of eight knots to the point where it intersects our course line at B. Then, using the same scale, we measure the distance from A to B and determine our speed over the bottom. With the protractor or parallel rule again, we check the angle of line C - B and have a heading necessary to maintain course.

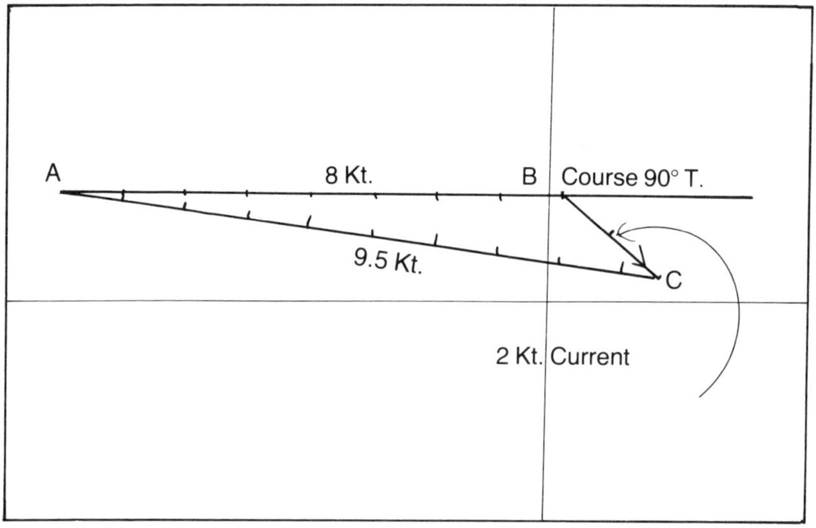

Figure 34a

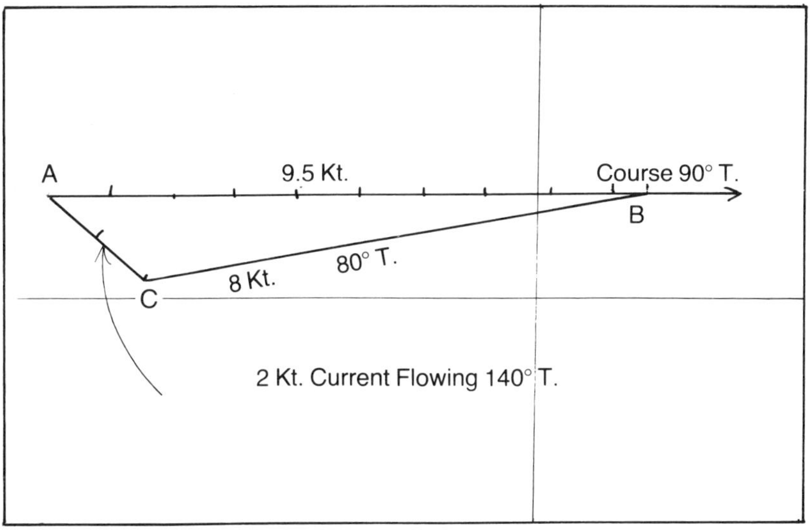

Figure 34b

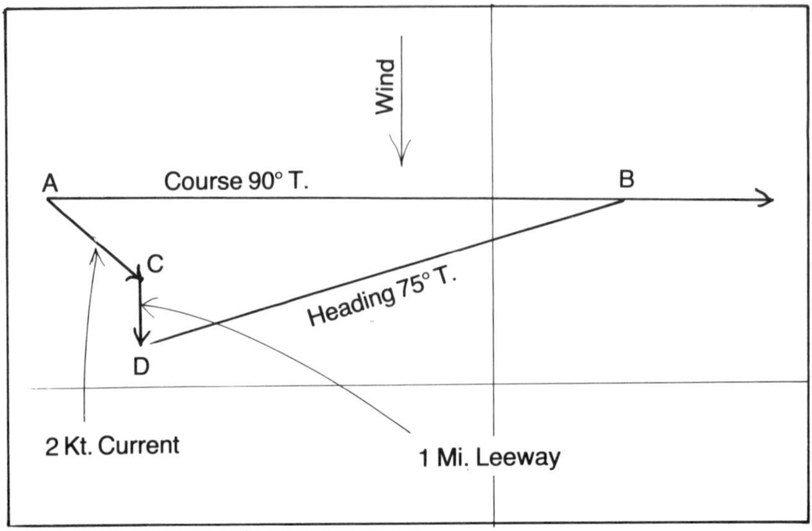

Figure 35a

81. LEEWAY

Leeway is different for each boat depending on the surface each presents to the wind, and the resistance the underwater profile presents to the water. A flat-bottomed, shallow draft, high-sided boat will drift downwind like a sled. A deep-keeled boat with a low superstructure will hold better against a beam wind. This is true whether it is a sail or a power boat. The sailboat always has a large piece of canvas *up* in the wind, but also has a keel *down* in the water. The skipper must come to know his own craft, and how it will behave in different conditions, to be able to predict leeway. Once predicted, it can be treated in the same manner as current. It can also be treated by learning the number of degrees of heading change into the wind necessary to offset the leeway.

Let's take a look at both methods of correction (Fig. 35a). In this illustration, for convenience, the course is still 90°, and the speed is still eight knots. We start at A and expect to be on course at B in one hour. The current flows 120° true at two knots. We draft that line to C. Now, from experience we estimate that in these wind conditions (wind from the north) we can expect to drift downwind one mile in one hour. Plotting that from C to D, we now measure off eight knots through the water back to the course line and find a heading necessary to maintain course. We can measure the length of line A - B and determine our speed over the bottom.

In Figure 35b we have a sailor who estimates his leeway by angle into the wind necessary to offset the error. Under these conditions, and with the same results, he will plot the current effect, measure his angle from C to B, and then allow 8° for leeway.

In the foregoing examples of current effect and correction, we have used one hour as the time reference, simply because it is used mostly to define boat speed, current speed, and wind speed. There is nothing magic about one hour. Any time reference can be used so long as it is used for all conditions. On a long crossing a twenty-four hour day may be more convenient. Pilot chart current information is recorded for twenty-four hours. When current and wind conditions are expected to change at specific times or places, it might be more convenient to make plots for the legs of a course from change to change.

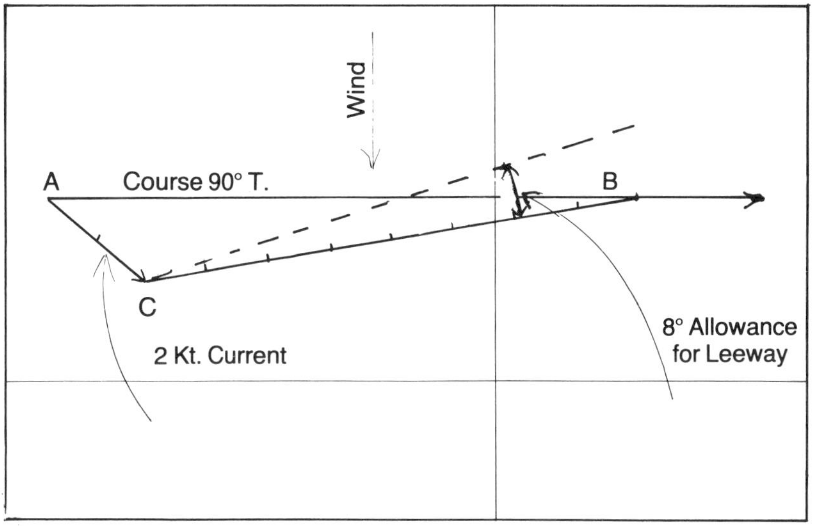

Figure 35b

82. FINDING CURRENT EFFECT BETWEEN FIXES

All of the foregoing concerning current presumes that you can accurately predict what the current will be. It would be ideal if this were the case, but even the Coast Pilot and pilot chart information is an approximation at best in most cruising waters. In practice you will usually be working the current problem after the fact and hoping it will apply to the immediate future. This is why DR position plots, as specifically defined in article 7, are important.

Remember what that definition was? Your DR position is the place where you would be if you, in fact, traveled in the direction you headed, traveled at the speed your instruments indicated (through the water) and for the time your watch tells you. Any difference between that position and a fix for the same time can be called current effect.

We can work the plot problems after the fact, and from the answer, determine the current as we go along. Let's work a problem and see how it goes.

We are returning to Honolulu from Lahaina in a cruising power boat. We left Lahaina at 1500 (3:00 P.M.) and went between Molokai and Lanai, "down the slot" as it is referred to by local sailors (Fig. 36). A little before 2000, we saw a glow from Honolulu in the sky and changed course to head for it. A check of position by bearings from the Molokai aero beacon and Laau Point light gives a fix, and a check with the chart gives a course of 290° true (279°M.) to the buoy off Diamond Head.

Soon, Laau Point and the aero beacon are out of sight astern, but by then the big bright light at Makapuu is up over the horizon ahead. We won't have Diamond Head light in view until we are about half way across the channel. We continue on a heading of 290° T, our compass reading 279° with no deviation on this heading. At 2200, some fifteen minutes before we expect it, Diamond Head light rises above the horizon. Waiting a few minutes until it is clear of the horizon we then take two quick bearings on it and Makapuu. We now record our DR at sixteen miles down the course from the fix off Molokai. We compute and

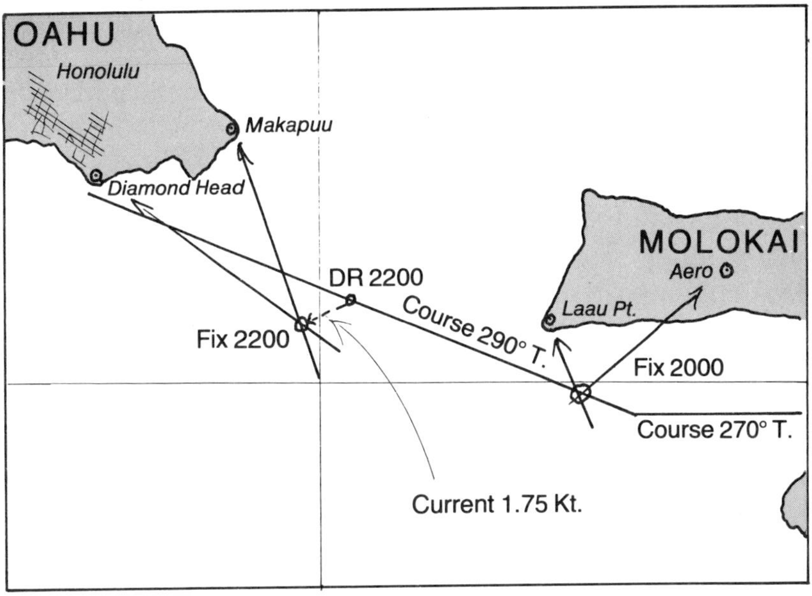

Figure 36

draft our bearings from Diamond Head and Makapuu, plot our fix and compare it with the DR. The distance and direction of the fix from the DR indicates the current has moved me forward and to the left of course. By measurement we determine that the current is a 1.75 knots current, as it has moved us three and a half miles in two hours. It is a west-southwest current. With it you are netting nine knots over the bottom. Now you can work out the problem of a new course from the 2200 fix to the buoy off Diamond Head. Assume that the current will continue, taking it into account when you plot the new course. Also, advance your ETA (estimated time of arrival) as you are making one knot more than you had expected.

83. ESTIMATED TIME OF ARRIVAL (ETA)

There may be instances when you want to arrive at a particular point at a particular time. This doesn't happen often with rag sailors (sailboat sailors), since time of arrival almost always depends on the wind over which they have no control. With power boaters there can be a schedule to meet, interceptions at sea to make, and log races to win, for example. Under such circumstances, being able to predict time accurately as related to distance is important. Here is a problem (Fig. 37) exemplifying this need:

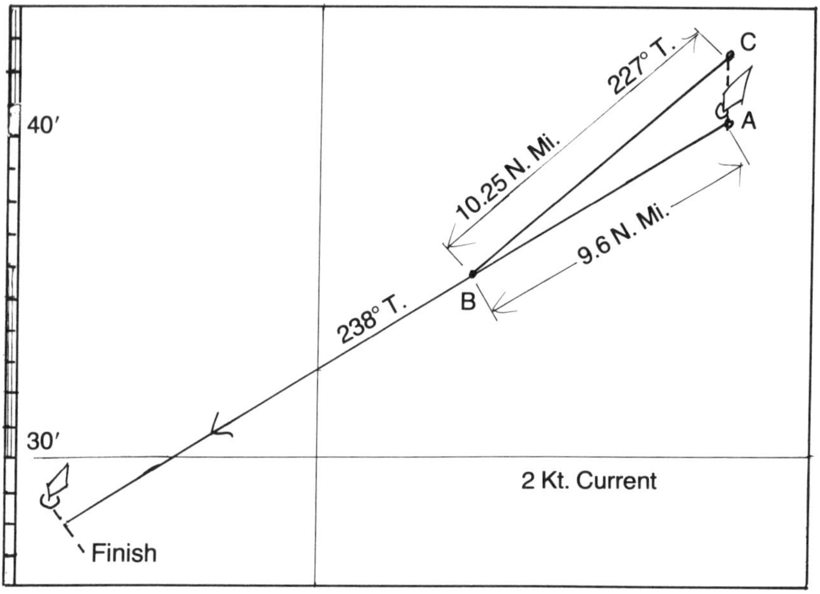

Figure 37

In this illustration you are in a navigators' race of some kind, you have rounded the buoy at sea, marked A in the upper right corner of the illustration. On your way out you suspect and confirm a current flowing north at two knots. You have to get back to the finish line in exactly two and a half hours. It is twenty-four miles away. Your cruiser has a maximum cruising speed of twelve knots. You know from experience and tests over a measured mile how to control speed by RPM setting. Therefore, what speed through the water must be maintained to cover the distance in exactly 2.5 hours?

First, you get a speed over the bottom. Divide the distance, 24 miles, by the time, 2.5 hours and find that you must make good 9.6 knots. Mark this off down the course line from the seaward buoy at B. Now, from A, plot the two-knot current to point C and measure the distance from there to B. You will find that you must travel at 10.25 knots through the water to net 9.6 knots over the bottom. Your base course from the buoy to the finish is 238°T. I measure the angle of the heading from C to B and find it to be 227°T. If the current holds I should finish in exactly two and one half hours. Now, that wasn't so bad was it?

EPILOGUE

IT WAS several years ago. Friends and I were hosting a Transpac boat in the forty-foot range. She was a new design and had been doing well most of the race which, except for *Windward Passage*, had been a light air event as Transpacs go. *Passage* got in before the wind faded and had wrapped up all the big boat and fleet silver. Our yacht had a chance for class honors, and we were hoping she would finish before noon of that final day.

We had cases of beer, gallons of mai tai, pupus by the bucketful and pounds and pounds of fruit all ready for the crew. We were prepared to meet them offshore with champagne. Hawaii doesn't stint on hosting. The call from headquarters at 7:30 A.M. gave an ETA of 10:00 A.M., and it looked like we were in the money.

I was acting as one of the many committee boats who meets the finishing yachts at the line and escorts them to their berth. I arranged to be assigned this yacht, and for someone to relieve me after she finished so that I could join in the festive occasion. We got our party gear ready and waited. We waited. And we waited. Finally at four in the afternoon she hove into view off Diamond Head. We gave her the party that we had planned and joined in the sorrow.

Some few mai tais later I was below looking over the navigator's plots. He was there and I asked him what had caused the delay after the early ETA.

"The Coast Guard," he exploded, "or whoever it is that arranges light sequences. Why would they use the same sequence on two lights so close together?"

"What do you mean?" I asked.

"That light on Molokai," he answered, "it has the same ten-second flash that Makapuu has. We radioed in our ETA in the middle of the night when we saw what we thought was Makapuu. We had to take down our chute and almost beat toward it for hours. It wasn't until dawn that we saw it was the light on Molokai. Why would they do that?"

I am normally a defender of the Coast Guard, but he was such an unhappy guy that I just shook my head and poured him another mai tai. I took a quick look at the chart to confirm my memory. It was good. Makapuu is a ten-second occulting light. The one on Molokai flashes every ten seconds. They are not at all alike. It appears that it can happen to the best of navigators. Don't let it happen to you.

APPENDIX

EXPLANATION OF TABLES

TABLE I

SPEED TABLE FOR MEASURED MILE

Before using this table, time two runs over a measured mile, running in opposite directions so as to offset any current, and average the two times. With this average, enter the table at the top or bottom with the number of minutes, and along either side with the number of seconds. The number from the table is speed in knots.

TABLE II

CONVERSION TABLE FOR NAUTICAL AND STATUTE MILES

The table is in two parts. The left hand portion is a conversion from nautical to statute, the right hand from statute to nautical. For distances longer than one hundred miles, the entering value can be multiplied by any power of ten. The corresponding factor must then be multiplied by the same power for conversion.

TABLE III

CONVERSION OF COMPASS POINTS TO DEGREES

Compass points to the quarter point are given along with the equivalent of degrees, minutes, and seconds.

TABLE IV

DISTANCE OF THE HORIZON

The table gives the distance to the horizon in nautical and statute miles. It is computed assuming standard atmospheric conditions. Nonstandard conditions, such as temperature and barometric pressure conditions, could introduce an error of a few tenths.

EXPLANATION OF TABLES

TABLE V
UNITS OF DEPTH MEASUREMENT ON CHARTS OF VARIOUS NATIONS

This gives the name of the sounding unit used by a number of maritime nations and its equivalent in feet.

TABLE VI
BEAUFORT SCALE WITH CORRESPONDING SEA STATE CODES

This gives Beaufort numbers and the wind speed range to which each number applies. Speeds are in all the usual measurement standards. Data descriptive of the effect that will be observed on land and sea is also included.

TABLE VII
CONVERSION TABLE FOR METERS, FEET, AND FATHOMS

Comparison is made using each measure as a base.

TABLE VIII
SPEED, TIME, AND DISTANCE

This table is entered either by speed in knots, from 0.5 to 16.0, or by time, in minutes, from 1 to 60. The answer obtained at the coordinates of speed and time will give the distance traveled. (The table in Bowditch includes speeds up to 40 knots.)

(Tables taken from Bowditch.)

TABLE I

Speed Table for Measured Mile

Sec.	Minutes 1	2	3	4	5	6	7	8	9	10	11	12	Sec.
	Knots	*Knots*	*Knots*	*Knots*	*Knots*	*Knots*	*Knots*	*Knots*	*Knots*	*Knots*	*Knots*	*Knots*	
0	60. 000	30. 000	20. 000	15. 000	12. 000	10. 000	8. 571	7. 500	6. 667	6. 000	5. 455	5. 000	0
1	59. 016	29. 752	19. 890	14. 938	11. 960	9. 972	8. 551	7. 484	6. 654	5. 990	5. 446	4. 993	1
2	58. 065	29. 508	19. 780	14. 876	11. 921	9. 945	8. 531	7. 469	6. 642	5. 980	5. 438	4. 986	2
3	57. 143	29. 268	19. 672	14. 815	11. 881	9. 917	8. 511	7. 453	6. 630	5. 970	5. 430	4. 979	3
4	56. 250	29. 032	19. 565	14. 754	11. 842	9. 890	8. 491	7. 438	6. 618	5. 960	5. 422	4. 972	4
5	55. 385	28. 800	19. 459	14. 694	11. 803	9. 863	8. 471	7. 423	6. 606	5. 950	5. 414	4. 966	5
6	54. 545	28. 571	19. 355	14. 634	11. 765	9. 836	8. 451	7. 407	6. 593	5. 941	5. 405	4. 959	6
7	53. 731	28. 346	19. 251	14. 575	11. 726	9. 809	8. 431	7. 392	6. 581	5. 931	5. 397	4. 952	7
8	52. 941	28. 125	19. 149	14. 516	11. 688	9. 783	8. 411	7. 377	6. 569	5. 921	5. 389	4. 945	8
9	52. 174	27. 907	19. 048	14. 458	11. 650	9. 756	8. 392	7. 362	6. 557	5. 911	5. 381	4. 938	9
10	51. 429	27. 692	18. 947	14. 400	11. 613	9. 730	8. 372	7. 347	6. 545	5. 902	5. 373	4. 932	10
11	50. 704	27. 481	18. 848	14. 343	11. 576	9. 704	8. 353	7. 332	6. 534	5. 892	5. 365	4. 925	11
12	50. 000	27. 273	18. 750	14. 286	11. 538	9. 677	8. 333	7. 317	6. 522	5. 882	5. 357	4. 918	12
13	49. 315	27. 068	18. 653	14. 229	11. 502	9. 651	8. 314	7. 302	6. 510	5. 873	5. 349	4. 911	13
14	48. 649	26. 866	18. 557	14. 173	11. 465	9. 626	8. 295	7. 287	6. 498	5. 863	5. 341	4. 905	14
15	48. 000	26. 667	18. 462	14. 118	11. 429	9. 600	8. 276	7. 273	6. 486	5. 854	5. 333	4. 898	15
16	47. 368	26. 471	18. 367	14. 062	11. 392	9. 574	8. 257	7. 258	6. 475	5. 844	5. 325	4. 891	16
17	46. 753	26. 277	18. 274	14. 008	11. 356	9. 549	8. 238	7. 243	6. 463	5. 835	5. 318	4. 885	17
18	46. 154	26. 087	18. 182	13. 953	11. 321	9. 524	8. 219	7. 229	6. 452	5. 825	5. 310	4. 878	18
19	45. 570	25. 899	18. 090	13. 900	11. 285	9. 499	8. 200	7. 214	6. 440	5. 816	5. 302	4. 871	19
20	45. 000	25. 714	18. 000	13. 846	11. 250	9. 474	8. 182	7. 200	6. 429	5. 806	5. 294	4. 865	20
21	44. 444	25. 532	17. 910	13. 793	11. 215	9. 449	8. 163	7. 186	6. 417	5. 797	5. 286	4. 858	21
22	43. 902	25. 352	17. 822	13. 740	11. 180	9. 424	8. 145	7. 171	6. 406	5. 788	5. 279	4. 852	22
23	43. 373	25. 175	17. 734	13. 688	11. 146	9. 399	8. 126	7. 157	6. 394	5. 778	5. 271	4. 845	23
24	42. 857	25. 000	17. 647	13. 636	11. 111	9. 375	8. 108	7. 143	6. 383	5. 769	5. 263	4. 839	24
25	42. 353	24. 828	17. 561	13. 585	11. 077	9. 351	8. 090	7. 129	6. 372	5. 760	5. 255	4. 832	25
26	41. 860	24. 658	17. 476	13. 534	11. 043	9. 326	8. 072	7. 115	6. 360	5. 751	5. 248	4. 826	26
27	41. 379	24. 490	17. 391	13. 483	11. 009	9. 302	8. 054	7. 101	6. 349	5. 742	5. 240	4. 819	27
28	40. 909	24. 324	17. 308	13. 433	10. 976	9. 278	8. 036	7. 087	6. 338	5. 732	5. 233	4. 813	28
29	40. 449	24. 161	17. 225	13. 383	10. 942	9. 254	8. 018	7. 073	6. 327	5. 723	5. 225	4. 806	29
30	40. 000	24. 000	17. 143	13. 333	10. 909	9. 231	8. 000	7. 059	6. 316	5. 714	5. 217	4. 800	30
31	39. 560	23. 841	17. 062	13. 284	10. 876	9. 207	7. 982	7. 045	6. 305	5. 705	5. 210	4. 794	31
32	39. 130	23. 684	16. 981	13. 235	10. 843	9. 184	7. 965	7. 031	6. 294	5. 696	5. 202	4. 787	32
33	38. 710	23. 529	16. 901	13. 187	10. 811	9. 160	7. 947	7. 018	6. 283	5. 687	5. 195	4. 781	33
34	38. 298	23. 377	16. 822	13. 139	10. 778	9. 137	7. 930	7. 004	6. 272	5. 678	5. 187	4. 775	34
35	37. 895	23. 226	16. 744	13. 091	10. 746	9. 114	7. 912	6. 990	6. 261	5. 669	5. 180	4. 768	35
36	37. 500	23. 077	16. 667	13. 043	10. 714	9. 091	7. 895	6. 977	6. 250	5. 660	5. 172	4. 762	36
37	37. 113	22. 930	16. 590	12. 996	10. 682	9. 068	7. 877	6. 963	6. 239	5. 651	5. 165	4. 756	37
38	36. 735	22. 785	16. 514	12. 950	10. 651	9. 045	7. 860	6. 950	6. 228	5. 643	5. 158	4. 749	38
39	36. 364	22. 642	16. 438	12. 903	10. 619	9. 023	7. 843	6. 936	6. 218	5. 634	5. 150	4. 743	39
40	36. 000	22. 500	16. 364	12. 857	10. 588	9. 000	7. 826	6. 923	6. 207	5. 625	5. 143	4. 737	40
41	35. 644	22. 360	16. 290	12. 811	10. 557	8. 978	7. 809	6. 910	6. 196	5. 616	5. 136	4. 731	41
42	35. 294	22. 222	16. 216	12. 766	10. 526	8. 955	7. 792	6. 897	6. 186	5. 607	5. 128	4. 724	42
43	34. 951	22. 086	16. 143	12. 721	10. 496	8. 933	7. 775	6. 883	6. 175	5. 599	5. 121	4. 718	43
44	34. 615	21. 951	16. 071	12. 676	10. 465	8. 911	7. 759	6. 870	6. 164	5. 590	5. 114	4. 712	44
45	34. 286	21. 818	16. 000	12. 632	10. 435	8. 889	7. 742	6. 857	6. 154	5. 581	5. 106	4. 706	45
46	33. 962	21. 687	15. 929	12. 587	10. 405	8. 867	7. 725	6. 844	6. 143	5. 573	5. 099	4. 700	46
47	33. 645	21. 557	15. 859	12. 544	10. 375	8. 845	7. 709	6. 831	6. 133	5. 564	5. 092	4. 694	47
48	33. 333	21. 429	15. 789	12. 500	10. 345	8. 824	7. 692	6. 818	6. 122	5. 556	5. 085	4. 688	48
49	33. 028	21. 302	15. 721	12. 457	10. 315	8. 802	7. 676	6. 805	6. 112	5. 547	5. 078	4. 681	49
50	32. 727	21. 176	15. 652	12. 414	10. 286	8. 780	7. 660	6. 792	6. 102	5. 538	5. 070	4. 675	50
51	32. 432	21. 053	15. 584	12. 371	10. 256	8. 759	7. 643	6. 780	6. 091	5. 530	5. 063	4. 669	51
52	32. 143	20. 930	15. 517	12. 329	10. 227	8. 738	7. 627	6. 767	6. 081	5. 521	5. 056	4. 663	52
53	31. 858	20. 809	15. 451	12. 287	10. 198	8. 717	7. 611	6. 754	6. 071	5. 513	5. 049	4. 657	53
54	31. 579	20. 690	15. 385	12. 245	10. 169	8. 696	7. 595	6. 742	6. 061	5. 505	5. 042	4. 651	54
55	31. 304	20. 571	15. 319	12. 203	10. 141	8. 675	7. 579	6. 729	6. 050	5. 496	5. 035	4. 645	55
56	31. 034	20. 455	15. 254	12. 162	10. 112	8. 654	7. 563	6. 716	6. 040	5. 488	5. 028	4. 639	56
57	30. 769	20. 339	15. 190	12. 121	10. 084	8. 633	7. 547	6. 704	6. 030	5. 479	5. 021	4. 633	57
58	30. 508	20. 225	15. 126	12. 081	10. 056	8. 612	7. 531	6. 691	6. 020	5. 471	5. 014	4. 627	58
59	30. 252	20. 112	15. 063	12. 040	10. 028	8. 592	7. 516	6. 679	6. 010	5. 463	5. 007	4. 621	59
60	30. 000	20. 000	15. 000	12. 000	10. 000	8. 571	7. 500	6. 667	6. 000	5. 455	5. 000	4. 615	60
Sec.	1	2	3	4	5	6	7	8	9	10	11	12	Sec.

TABLE II

Conversion Table for Nautical and Statute Miles

1 nautical mile=6,076.11548 . . . feet

1 statute mile=5,280 feet

Nautical miles to statute miles				Statute miles to nautical miles			
Nautical miles	Statute miles	Nautical miles	Statute miles	Statute miles	Nautical miles	Statute miles	Nautical miles
1	1. 151	51	58. 690	1	0. 869	51	44. 318
2	2. 302	52	59. 841	2	1. 738	52	45. 187
3	3. 452	53	60. 991	3	2. 607	53	46. 056
4	4. 603	54	62. 142	4	3. 476	54	46. 925
5	5. 754	55	63. 293	5	4. 345	55	47. 794
6	6. 905	56	64. 444	6	5. 214	56	48. 663
7	8. 055	57	65. 594	7	6. 083	57	49. 532
8	9. 206	58	66. 745	8	6. 952	58	50. 401
9	10. 357	59	67. 896	9	7. 821	59	51. 270
10	11. 508	60	69. 047	10	8. 690	60	52. 139
11	12. 659	61	70. 198	11	9. 559	61	53. 008
12	13. 809	62	71. 348	12	10. 428	62	53. 877
13	14. 960	63	72. 499	13	11. 297	63	54. 746
14	16. 111	64	73. 650	14	12. 166	64	55. 614
15	17. 262	65	74. 801	15	13. 035	65	56. 483
16	18. 412	66	75. 951	16	13. 904	66	57. 352
17	19. 563	67	77. 102	17	14. 773	67	58. 221
18	20. 714	68	78. 253	18	15. 642	68	59. 090
19	21. 865	69	79. 404	19	16. 511	69	59. 959
20	23. 016	70	80. 555	20	17. 380	70	60. 828
21	24. 166	71	81. 705	21	18. 249	71	61. 697
22	25. 317	72	82. 856	22	19. 117	72	62. 566
23	26. 468	73	84. 007	23	19. 986	73	63. 435
24	27. 619	74	85. 158	24	20. 855	74	64. 304
25	28. 769	75	86. 308	25	21. 724	75	65. 173
26	29. 920	76	87. 459	26	22. 593	76	66. 042
27	31. 071	77	88. 610	27	23. 462	77	66. 911
28	32. 222	78	89. 761	28	24. 331	78	67. 780
29	33. 373	79	90. 912	29	25. 200	79	68. 649
30	34. 523	80	92. 062	30	26. 069	80	69. 518
31	35. 674	81	93. 213	31	26. 938	81	70. 387
32	36. 825	82	94. 364	32	27. 807	82	71. 256
33	37. 976	83	95. 515	33	28. 676	83	72. 125
34	39. 127	84	96. 665	34	29. 545	84	72. 994
35	40. 277	85	97. 816	35	30. 414	85	73. 863
36	41. 428	86	98. 967	36	31. 283	86	74. 732
37	42. 579	87	100. 118	37	32. 152	87	75. 601
38	43. 730	88	101. 269	38	33. 021	88	76. 470
39	44. 880	89	102. 419	39	33. 890	89	77. 339
40	46. 031	90	103. 570	40	34. 759	90	78. 208
41	47. 182	91	104. 721	41	35. 628	91	79. 077
42	48. 333	92	105. 872	42	36. 497	92	79. 946
43	49. 484	93	107. 022	43	37. 366	93	80. 815
44	50. 634	94	108. 173	44	38. 235	94	81. 684
45	51. 785	95	109. 324	45	39. 104	95	82. 553
46	52. 936	96	110. 475	46	39. 973	96	83. 422
47	54. 087	97	111. 626	47	40. 842	97	84. 291
48	55. 237	98	112. 776	48	41. 711	98	85. 160
49	56. 388	99	113. 927	49	42. 580	99	86. 029
50	57. 539	100	115. 078	50	43. 449	100	86. 898

TABLE III

Conversion of Compass Points to Degrees

	Points	Angular measure ° ′ ″
NORTH TO EAST		
North	0	0 00 00
N¼E	¼	2 48 45
N½E	½	5 37 30
N¾E	¾	8 26 15
N by E	1	11 15 00
N by E¼E	1¼	14 03 45
N by E½E	1½	16 52 30
N by E¾E	1¾	19 41 15
NNE	2	22 30 00
NNE¼E	2¼	25 18 45
NNE½E	2½	28 07 30
NNE¾E	2¾	30 56 15
NE by N	3	33 45 00
NE¾N	3¼	36 33 45
NE½N	3½	39 22 30
NE¼N	3¾	42 11 15
NE	4	45 00 00
NE¼E	4¼	47 48 45
NE½E	4½	50 37 30
NE¾E	4¾	53 26 15
NE by E	5	56 15 00
NE by E¼E	5¼	59 03 45
NE by E½E	5½	61 52 30
NE by E¾E	5¾	64 41 15
ENE	6	67 30 00
ENE¼E	6¼	70 18 45
ENE½E	6½	73 07 30
ENE¾E	6¾	75 56 15
E by N	7	78 45 00
E¾N	7¼	81 33 45
E½N	7½	84 22 30
E¼N	7¾	87 11 15
EAST TO SOUTH		
East	8	90 00 00
E¼S	8¼	92 48 45
E½S	8½	95 37 30
E¾S	8¾	98 26 15
E by S	9	101 15 00
ESE¾E	9¼	104 03 45
ESE½E	9½	106 52 30
ESE¼E	9¾	109 41 15
ESE	10	112 30 00
SE by E¾E	10¼	115 18 45
SE by E½E	10½	118 07 30
SE by E¼E	10¾	120 56 15
SE by E	11	123 45 00
SE¾E	11¼	126 33 45
SE½E	11½	129 22 30
SE¼E	11¾	132 11 15
SE	12	135 00 00
SE¼S	12¼	137 48 45
SE½S	12½	140 37 30
SE¾S	12¾	143 26 15
SE by S	13	146 15 00
SSE¾E	13¼	149 03 45
SSE½E	13½	151 52 30
SSE¼E	13¾	154 41 15
SSE	14	157 30 00
S by E¾E	14¼	160 18 45
S by E½E	14½	163 07 30
S by E¼E	14¾	165 56 15
S by E	15	168 45 00
S¾E	15¼	171 33 45
S½E	15½	174 22 30
S¼E	15¾	177 11 15
South	16	180 00 00
SOUTH TO WEST		
South	16	180 00 00
S¼W	16¼	182 48 45
S½W	16½	185 37 30
S¾W	16¾	188 26 15
S by W	17	191 15 00
S by W¼W	17¼	194 03 45
S by W½W	17½	196 52 30
S by W¾W	17¾	199 41 15
SSW	18	202 30 00
SSW¼W	18¼	205 18 45
SSW½W	18½	208 07 30
SSW¾W	18¾	210 56 15
SW by S	19	213 45 00
SW¾S	19¼	216 33 45
SW½S	19½	219 22 30
SW¼S	19¾	222 11 15
SW	20	225 00 00
SW¼W	20¼	227 48 45
SW½W	20½	230 37 30
SW¾W	20¾	233 26 15
SW by W	21	236 15 00
SW by W¼W	21¼	239 03 45
SW by W½W	21½	241 52 30
SW by W¾W	21¾	244 41 15
WSW	22	247 30 00
WSW¼W	22¼	250 18 45
WSW½W	22½	253 07 30
WSW¾W	22¾	255 56 15
W by S	23	258 45 00
W¾S	23¼	261 33 45
W½S	23½	264 22 30
W¼S	23¾	267 11 15
WEST TO NORTH		
West	24	270 00 00
W¼N	24¼	272 48 45
W½N	24½	275 37 30
W¾N	24¾	278 26 15
W by N	25	281 15 00
WNW¾W	25¼	284 03 45
WNW½W	25½	286 52 30
WNW¼W	25¾	289 41 15
WNW	26	292 30 00
NW by W¾W	26¼	295 18 45
NW by W½W	26½	298 07 30
NW by W¼W	26¾	300 56 15
NW by W	27	303 45 00
NW¾W	27¼	306 33 45
NW½W	27½	309 22 30
NW¼W	27¾	312 11 15
NW	28	315 00 00
NW¼N	28¼	317 48 45
NW½N	28½	320 37 30
NW¾N	28¾	323 26 15
NW by N	29	326 15 00
NNW¾W	29¼	329 03 45
NNW½W	29½	331 52 30
NNW¼W	29¾	334 41 15
NNW	30	337 30 00
N by W¾W	30¼	340 18 45
N by W½W	30½	343 07 30
N by W¼W	30¾	345 56 15
N by W	31	348 45 00
N¾W	31¼	351 33 45
N½W	31½	354 22 30
N¼W	31¾	357 11 15
North	32	360 00 00

TABLE IV
Distance of the Horizon

Height feet	Nautical miles	Statute miles	Height feet	Nautical miles	Statute miles	Height feet	Nautical miles	Statute miles
1	1. 1	1. 3	120	12. 5	14. 4	940	35. 1	40. 4
2	1. 6	1. 9	125	12. 8	14. 7	960	35. 4	40. 8
3	2. 0	2. 3	130	13. 0	15. 0	980	35. 8	41. 2
4	2. 3	2. 6	135	13. 3	15. 3	1, 000	36. 2	41. 6
5	2. 6	2. 9	140	13. 5	15. 6	1, 100	37. 9	43. 7
6	2. 8	3. 2	145	13. 8	15. 9	1, 200	39. 6	45. 6
7	3. 0	3. 5	150	14. 0	16. 1	1, 300	41. 2	47. 5
8	3. 2	3. 7	160	14. 5	16. 7	1, 400	42. 8	49. 3
9	3. 4	4. 0	170	14. 9	17. 2	1, 500	44. 3	51. 0
10	3. 6	4. 2	180	15. 3	17. 7	1, 600	45. 8	52. 7
11	3. 8	4. 4	190	15. 8	18. 2	1, 700	47. 2	54. 3
12	4. 0	4. 6	200	16. 2	18. 6	1, 800	48. 5	55. 9
13	4. 1	4. 7	210	16. 6	19. 1	1, 900	49. 9	57. 4
14	4. 3	4. 9	220	17. 0	19. 5	2, 000	51. 2	58. 9
15	4. 4	5. 1	230	17. 3	20. 0	2, 100	52. 4	60. 4
16	4. 6	5. 3	240	17. 7	20. 4	2, 200	53. 7	61. 8
17	4. 7	5. 4	250	18. 1	20. 8	2, 300	54. 9	63. 2
18	4. 9	5. 6	260	18. 4	21. 2	2, 400	56. 0	64. 5
19	5. 0	5. 7	270	18. 8	21. 6	2, 500	57. 2	65. 8
20	5. 1	5. 9	280	19. 1	22. 0	2, 600	58. 3	67. 2
21	5. 2	6. 0	290	19. 5	22. 4	2, 700	59. 4	68. 4
22	5. 4	6. 2	300	19. 8	22. 8	2, 800	60. 5	69. 7
23	5. 5	6. 3	310	20. 1	23. 2	2, 900	61. 6	70. 9
24	5. 6	6. 5	320	20. 5	23. 6	3, 000	62. 7	72. 1
25	5. 7	6. 6	330	20. 8	23. 9	3, 100	63. 7	73. 3
26	5. 8	6. 7	340	21. 1	24. 3	3, 200	64. 7	74. 5
27	5. 9	6. 8	350	21. 4	24. 6	3, 300	65. 7	75. 7
28	6. 1	7. 0	360	21. 7	25. 0	3, 400	66. 7	76. 8
29	6. 2	7. 1	370	22. 0	25. 3	3, 500	67. 7	77. 9
30	6. 3	7. 2	380	22. 3	25. 7	3, 600	68. 6	79. 0
31	6. 4	7. 3	390	22. 6	26. 0	3, 700	69. 6	80. 1
32	6. 5	7. 5	400	22. 9	26. 3	3, 800	70. 5	81. 2
33	6. 6	7. 6	410	23. 2	26. 7	3, 900	71. 4	82. 2
34	6. 7	7. 7	420	23. 4	27. 0	4, 000	72. 4	83. 3
35	6. 8	7. 8	430	23. 7	27. 3	4, 100	73. 3	84. 3
36	6. 9	7. 9	440	24. 0	27. 6	4, 200	74. 1	85. 4
37	7. 0	8. 0	450	24. 3	27. 9	4, 300	75. 0	86. 4
38	7. 1	8. 1	460	24. 5	28. 2	4, 400	75. 9	87. 4
39	7. 1	8. 2	470	24. 8	28. 6	4, 500	76. 7	88. 3
40	7. 2	8. 3	480	25. 1	28. 9	4, 600	77. 6	89. 3
41	7. 3	8. 4	490	25. 3	29. 2	4, 700	78. 4	90. 3
42	7. 4	8. 5	500	25. 6	29. 4	4, 800	79. 3	91. 2
43	7. 5	8. 6	520	26. 1	30. 0	4, 900	80. 1	92. 2
44	7. 6	8. 7	540	26. 6	30. 6	5, 000	80. 9	93. 1
45	7. 7	8. 8	560	27. 1	31. 2	6, 000	88. 6	102. 0
46	7. 8	8. 9	580	27. 6	31. 7	7, 000	95. 7	110. 2
47	7. 8	9. 0	600	28. 0	32. 3	8, 000	102. 3	117. 8
48	7. 9	9. 1	620	28. 5	32. 8	9, 000	108. 5	124. 9
49	8. 0	9. 2	640	28. 9	33. 3	10, 000	114. 4	131. 7
50	8. 1	9. 3	660	29. 4	33. 8	15, 000	140. 1	161. 3
55	8. 5	9. 8	680	29. 8	34. 3	20, 000	161. 8	186. 3
60	8. 9	10. 2	700	30. 3	34. 8	25, 000	180. 9	208. 2
65	9. 2	10. 6	720	30. 7	35. 3	30, 000	198. 1	228. 1
70	9. 6	11. 0	740	31. 1	35. 8	35, 000	214. 0	246. 4
75	9. 9	11. 4	760	31. 5	36. 3	40, 000	228. 8	263. 4
80	10. 2	11. 8	780	31. 9	36. 8	45, 000	242. 7	279. 4
85	10. 5	12. 1	800	32. 4	37. 3	50, 000	255. 8	294. 5
90	10. 9	12. 5	820	32. 8	37. 7	60, 000	280. 2	322. 6
95	11. 2	12. 8	840	33. 2	38. 2	70, 000	302. 7	348. 4
100	11. 4	13. 2	860	33. 5	38. 6	80, 000	323. 6	372. 5
105	11. 7	13. 5	880	33. 9	39. 1	90, 000	343. 2	395. 1
110	12. 0	13. 8	900	34. 3	39. 5	100, 000	361. 8	416. 5
115	12. 3	14. 1	920	34. 7	39. 9	200, 000	511. 6	589. 0

TABLE V
Units of Depth Measurement on Charts of Various Nations

Nation	Unit of depth measurement	Equivalent in United States units	
		Feet	Fathoms
Argentina	Braza	6.000	1.000
Australia	Fathom	6.000	1.000
Belgium	Metre	3.281	0.547
Brazil	Metro	3.281	0.547
Canada	Fathom	6.000	1.000
Chile	Metro	3.281	0.547
Denmark	Favn	6.176	1.029
	Meter	3.281	0.547
Finland	Metre	3.281	0.547
France	Metre	3.281	0.547
Germany	Meter	3.281	0.547
Great Britain	Fathom	6.000	1.000
Greece	Metre (Metpa)	3.281	0.547
Italy	Metre	3.281	0.547
Japan	Metre	3.281	0.547
Netherlands	Vadem	5.905	0.984
	Meter	3.281	0.547
Norway	Favn	6.176	1.029
	Meter	3.281	0.547
Portugal	Metro	3.281	0.547
Russia (USSR)	Sazhen'	6.000	1.000
	Metrc	3.281	0.547
Thailand	Metre	3.281	0.547
Spain	Metro	3.281	0.547
Sweden	Famn	5.844	0.974
	Meter	3.281	0.547
Turkey	Fathom (Kulac)	6.000	1.000
Uruguay	Metro	3.281	0.547
Yugoslavia	Metar	3.281	0.547

TABLE VI

Beaufort Scale with Corresponding Sea State Codes

Beaufort number	Wind speed: knots	Wind speed: mph	Wind speed: meters per second	Wind speed: km per hour	Seaman's term	World Meteorological Organization (1964)	Estimating wind speed: Effects observed at sea	Estimating wind speed: Effects observed on land	Hydrographic Office: Term and height of waves, in feet	Hydrographic Office: Code	World Meteorological Organization: Term and height of waves, in feet	World Meteorological Organization: Code
0	under 1	under 1	0. 0–0. 2	under 1	Calm	Calm	Sea like mirror.	Calm; smoke rises vertically.	Calm, 0	0	Calm, glassy, 0	0
1	1–3	1–3	0. 3–1. 5	1–5	Light air	Light air	Ripples with appearance of scales; no foam crests.	Smoke drift indicates wind direction; vanes do not move.	Smooth, less than 1	1		
2	4–6	4–7	1. 6–3. 3	6–11	Light breeze	Light breeze	Small wavelets; crests of glassy appearance, not breaking.	Wind felt on face; leaves rustle; vanes begin to move.	Slight, 1–3	2	Calm, rippled, 0–⅓	1
3	7–10	8–12	3. 4–5. 4	12–19	Gentle breeze	Gentle breeze	Large wavelets; crests begin to break; scattered whitecaps.	Leaves, small twigs in constant motion; light flags extended.	Moderate, 3–5	3	Smooth, wavelets, ⅓–1⅔	2
4	11–16	13–18	5. 5–7. 9	20–28	Moderate breeze	Moderate breeze	Small waves, becoming longer; numerous whitecaps.	Dust, leaves, and loose paper raised up; small branches move.			Slight, 2–4	3
5	17–21	19–24	8. 0–10. 7	29–38	Fresh breeze	Fresh breeze	Moderate waves, taking longer form; many whitecaps; some spray.	Small trees in leaf begin to sway.	Rough, 5–8	4	Moderate, 4–8	4
6	22–27	25–31	10. 8–13. 8	39–49	Strong breeze	Strong breeze	Larger waves forming; whitecaps everywhere; more spray.	Larger branches of trees in motion; whistling heard in wires.			Rough, 8–13	5
7	28–33	32–38	13. 9–17. 1	50–61	Moderate gale	Near gale	Sea heaps up; white foam from breaking waves begins to be blown in streaks.	Whole trees in motion; resistance felt in walking against wind.				
8	34–40	39–46	17. 2–20. 7	62–74	Fresh gale	Gale	Moderately high waves of greater length; edges of crests begin to break into spindrift; foam is blown in well-marked streaks.	Twigs and small branches broken off trees; progress generally impeded.	Very rough, 8–12	5	Very rough, 13–20	6
9	41–47	47–54	20. 8–24. 4	75–88	Strong gale	Strong gale	High waves; sea begins to roll; dense streaks of foam; spray may reduce visibility.	Slight structural damage occurs; slate blown from roofs.	High, 12–20	6		
10	48–55	55–63	24. 5–28. 4	89–102	Whole gale	Storm	Very high waves with overhanging crests; sea takes white appearance as foam is blown in very dense streaks; rolling is heavy and visibility reduced.	Seldom experienced on land; trees broken or uprooted; considerable structural damage occurs.	Very high, 20–40	7	High, 20–30	7
11	56–63	64–72	28. 5–32. 6	103–117	Storm	Violent storm	Exceptionally high waves; sea covered with white foam patches; visibility still more reduced.		Mountainous, 40 and higher	8	Very high, 30–45	8
12 13 14 15 16 17	64–71 72–80 81–89 90–99 100–108 109–118	73–82 83–92 93–103 104–114 115–125 126–136	32. 7–36. 9 37. 0–41. 4 41. 5–46. 1 46. 2–50. 9 51. 0–56. 0 56. 1–61. 2	118–133 134–149 150–166 167–183 184–201 202–220	Hurricane	Hurricane	Air filled with foam; sea completely white with driving spray; visibility greatly reduced.	Very rarely experienced on land; usually accompanied by widespread damage.	Confused	9	Phenomenal, over 45	9

Note: Since January 1, 1955, weather map symbols have been based upon wind speed in knots, at five-knot intervals, rather than upon Beaufort number.

TABLE VII

Conversion Table for Meters, Feet, and Fathoms

Meters	Feet	Fathoms	Meters	Feet	Fathoms	Feet	Meters	Feet	Meters	Fathoms	Meters	Fathoms	Meters
1	3. 28	0. 55	61	200. 13	33. 36	1	0. 30	61	18. 59	1	1. 83	61	111. 56
2	6. 56	1. 09	62	203. 41	33. 90	2	0. 61	62	18. 90	2	3. 66	62	113. 39
3	9. 84	1. 64	63	206. 69	34. 45	3	0. 91	63	19. 20	3	5. 49	63	115. 21
4	13. 12	2. 19	64	209. 97	35. 00	4	1. 22	64	19. 51	4	7. 32	64	117. 04
5	16. 40	2. 73	65	213. 25	35. 54	5	1. 52	65	19. 81	5	9. 14	65	118. 87
6	19. 69	3. 28	66	216. 54	36. 09	6	1. 83	66	20. 12	6	10. 97	66	120. 70
7	22. 97	3. 83	67	219. 82	36. 64	7	2. 13	67	20. 42	7	12. 80	67	122. 53
8	26. 25	4. 37	68	223. 10	37. 18	8	2. 44	68	20. 73	8	14. 63	68	124. 36
9	29. 53	4. 92	69	226. 38	37. 73	9	2. 74	69	21. 03	9	16. 46	69	126. 19
10	32. 81	5. 47	70	229. 66	38. 28	10	3. 05	70	21. 34	10	18. 29	70	128. 02
11	36. 09	6. 01	71	232. 94	38. 82	11	3. 35	71	21. 64	11	20. 12	71	129. 84
12	39. 37	6. 56	72	236. 22	39. 37	12	3. 66	72	21. 95	12	21. 95	72	131. 67
13	42. 65	7. 11	73	239. 50	39. 92	13	3. 96	73	22. 25	13	23. 77	73	133. 50
14	45. 93	7. 66	74	242. 78	40. 46	14	4. 27	74	22. 56	14	25. 60	74	135. 33
15	49. 21	8. 20	75	246. 06	41. 01	15	4. 57	75	22. 86	15	27. 43	75	137. 16
16	52. 49	8. 75	76	249. 34	41. 56	16	4. 88	76	23. 16	16	29. 26	76	138. 99
17	55. 77	9. 30	77	252. 62	42. 10	17	5. 18	77	23. 47	17	31. 09	77	140. 82
18	59. 06	9. 84	78	255. 91	42. 65	18	5. 49	78	23. 77	18	32. 92	78	142. 65
19	62. 34	10. 39	79	259. 19	43. 20	19	5. 79	79	24. 08	19	34. 75	79	144. 48
20	65. 62	10. 94	80	262. 47	43. 74	20	6. 10	80	24. 38	20	36. 58	80	146. 30
21	68. 90	11. 48	81	265. 75	44. 29	21	6. 40	81	24. 69	21	38. 40	81	148. 13
22	72. 18	12. 03	82	269. 03	44. 84	22	6. 71	82	24. 99	22	40. 23	82	149. 96
23	75. 46	12. 58	83	272. 31	45. 38	23	7. 01	83	25. 30	23	42. 06	83	151. 79
24	78. 74	13. 12	84	275. 59	45. 93	24	7. 32	84	25. 60	24	43. 89	84	153. 62
25	82. 02	13. 67	85	278. 87	46. 48	25	7. 62	85	25. 91	25	45. 72	85	155. 45
26	85. 30	14. 22	86	282. 15	47. 03	26	7. 92	86	26. 21	26	47. 55	86	157. 28
27	88. 58	14. 76	87	285. 43	47. 57	27	8. 23	87	26. 52	27	49. 38	87	159. 11
28	91. 86	15. 31	88	288. 71	48. 12	28	8. 53	88	26. 82	28	51. 21	88	160. 93
29	95. 14	15. 86	89	291. 99	48. 67	29	8. 84	89	27. 13	29	53. 04	89	162. 76
30	98. 43	16. 40	90	295. 28	49. 21	30	9. 14	90	27. 43	30	54. 86	90	164. 59
31	101. 71	16. 95	91	298. 56	49. 76	31	9. 45	91	27. 74	31	56. 69	91	166. 42
32	104. 99	17. 50	92	301. 84	50. 31	32	9. 75	92	28. 04	32	58. 52	92	168. 25
33	108. 27	18. 04	93	305. 12	50. 85	33	10. 06	93	28. 35	33	60. 35	93	170. 08
34	111. 55	18. 59	94	308. 40	51. 40	34	10. 36	94	28. 65	34	62. 18	94	171. 91
35	114. 83	19. 14	95	311. 68	51. 95	35	10. 67	95	28. 96	35	64. 01	95	173. 74
36	118. 11	19. 69	96	314. 96	52. 49	36	10. 97	96	29. 26	36	65. 84	96	175. 56
37	121. 39	20. 23	97	318. 24	53. 04	37	11. 28	97	29. 57	37	67. 67	97	177. 39
38	124. 67	20. 78	98	321. 52	53. 59	38	11. 58	98	29. 87	38	69. 49	98	179. 22
39	127. 95	21. 33	99	324. 80	54. 13	39	11. 89	99	30. 18	39	71. 32	99	181. 05
40	131. 23	21. 87	100	328. 08	54. 68	40	12. 19	100	30. 48	40	73. 15	100	182. 88
41	134. 51	22. 42	101	331. 36	55. 23	41	12. 50	101	30. 78	41	74. 98	101	184. 71
42	137. 80	22. 97	102	334. 65	55. 77	42	12. 80	102	31. 09	42	76. 81	102	186. 54
43	141. 08	23. 51	103	337. 93	56. 32	43	13. 11	103	31. 39	43	78. 64	103	188. 37
44	144. 36	24. 06	104	341. 21	56. 87	44	13. 41	104	31. 70	44	80. 47	104	190. 20
45	147. 64	24. 61	105	344. 49	57. 41	45	13. 72	105	32. 00	45	82. 30	105	192. 02
46	150. 92	25. 15	106	347. 77	57. 96	46	14. 02	106	32. 31	46	84. 12	106	193. 85
47	154. 20	25. 70	107	351. 05	58. 51	47	14. 33	107	32. 61	47	85. 95	107	195. 68
48	157. 48	26. 25	108	354. 33	59. 06	48	14. 63	108	32. 92	48	87. 78	108	197. 51
49	160. 76	26. 79	109	357. 61	59. 60	49	14. 94	109	33. 22	49	89. 61	109	199. 34
50	164. 04	27. 34	110	360. 89	60. 15	50	15. 24	110	33. 53	50	91. 44	110	201. 17
51	167. 32	27. 89	111	364. 17	60. 70	51	15. 54	111	33. 83	51	93. 27	111	203. 00
52	170. 60	28. 43	112	367. 45	61. 24	52	15. 85	112	34. 14	52	95. 10	112	204. 83
53	173. 88	28. 98	113	370. 73	61. 79	53	16. 15	113	34. 44	53	96. 93	113	206. 65
54	177. 17	29. 53	114	374. 02	62. 34	54	16. 46	114	34. 75	54	98. 76	114	208. 48
55	180. 45	30. 07	115	377. 30	62. 88	55	16. 76	115	35. 05	55	100. 58	115	210. 31
56	183. 73	30. 62	116	380. 58	63. 43	56	17. 07	116	35. 36	56	102. 41	116	212. 14
57	187. 01	31. 17	117	383. 86	63. 98	57	17. 37	117	35. 66	57	104. 24	117	213. 97
58	190. 29	31. 71	118	387. 14	64. 52	58	17. 68	118	35. 97	58	106. 07	118	215. 80
59	193. 57	32. 26	119	390. 42	65. 07	59	17. 98	119	36. 27	59	107. 90	119	217. 63
60	196. 85	32. 81	120	393. 70	65. 62	60	18. 29	120	36. 58	60	109. 73	120	219. 46

TABLE VIII
Speed, Time, and Distance

Minutes	Speed in knots																Minutes
	0.5	1.0	1.5	2.0	2.5	3.0	3.5	4.0	4.5	5.0	5.5	6.0	6.5	7.0	7.5	8.0	
	Miles	*Miles*	*Miles*	*Miles*	*Miles*	*Miles*	*Miles*	*Miles*	*Miles*	*Miles*	*Miles*	*Miles*	*Miles*	*Miles*	*Miles*	*Miles*	
1	0.0	0.0	0.0	0.0	0.0	0.0	0.1	0.1	0.1	0.1	0.1	0.1	0.1	0.1	0.1	0.1	1
2	0.0	0.0	0.0	0.1	0.1	0.1	0.1	0.1	0.2	0.2	0.2	0.2	0.2	0.2	0.2	0.3	2
3	0.0	0.0	0.1	0.1	0.1	0.2	0.2	0.2	0.2	0.2	0.3	0.3	0.3	0.4	0.4	0.4	3
4	0.0	0.1	0.1	0.1	0.2	0.2	0.2	0.3	0.3	0.3	0.4	0.4	0.4	0.5	0.5	0.5	4
5	0.0	0.1	0.1	0.2	0.2	0.2	0.3	0.3	0.4	0.4	0.5	0.5	0.5	0.6	0.6	0.7	5
6	0.0	0.1	0.2	0.2	0.2	0.3	0.4	0.4	0.4	0.5	0.6	0.6	0.6	0.7	0.8	0.8	6
7	0.1	0.1	0.2	0.2	0.3	0.4	0.4	0.5	0.5	0.6	0.6	0.7	0.8	0.8	0.9	0.9	7
8	0.1	0.1	0.2	0.3	0.3	0.4	0.5	0.5	0.6	0.7	0.7	0.8	0.9	0.9	1.0	1.1	8
9	0.1	0.2	0.2	0.3	0.4	0.4	0.5	0.6	0.7	0.8	0.8	0.9	1.0	1.0	1.1	1.2	9
10	0.1	0.2	0.2	0.3	0.4	0.5	0.6	0.7	0.8	0.8	0.9	1.0	1.1	1.2	1.2	1.3	10
11	0.1	0.2	0.3	0.4	0.5	0.6	0.6	0.7	0.8	0.9	1.0	1.1	1.2	1.3	1.4	1.5	11
12	0.1	0.2	0.3	0.4	0.5	0.6	0.7	0.8	0.9	1.0	1.1	1.2	1.3	1.4	1.5	1.6	12
13	0.1	0.2	0.3	0.4	0.5	0.6	0.8	0.9	1.0	1.1	1.2	1.3	1.4	1.5	1.6	1.7	13
14	0.1	0.2	0.4	0.5	0.6	0.7	0.8	0.9	1.0	1.2	1.3	1.4	1.5	1.6	1.8	1.9	14
15	0.1	0.2	0.4	0.5	0.6	0.8	0.9	1.0	1.1	1.2	1.4	1.5	1.6	1.8	1.9	2.0	15
16	0.1	0.3	0.4	0.5	0.7	0.8	0.9	1.1	1.2	1.3	1.5	1.6	1.7	1.9	2.0	2.1	16
17	0.1	0.3	0.4	0.6	0.7	0.8	1.0	1.1	1.3	1.4	1.6	1.7	1.8	2.0	2.1	2.3	17
18	0.2	0.3	0.4	0.6	0.8	0.9	1.0	1.2	1.4	1.5	1.6	1.8	2.0	2.1	2.2	2.4	18
19	0.2	0.3	0.5	0.6	0.8	1.0	1.1	1.3	1.4	1.6	1.7	1.9	2.1	2.2	2.4	2.5	19
20	0.2	0.3	0.5	0.7	0.8	1.0	1.2	1.3	1.5	1.7	1.8	2.0	2.2	2.3	2.5	2.7	20
21	0.2	0.4	0.5	0.7	0.9	1.0	1.2	1.4	1.6	1.8	1.9	2.1	2.3	2.4	2.6	2.8	21
22	0.2	0.4	0.6	0.7	0.9	1.1	1.3	1.5	1.6	1.8	2.0	2.2	2.4	2.6	2.8	2.9	22
23	0.2	0.4	0.6	0.8	1.0	1.2	1.3	1.5	1.7	1.9	2.1	2.3	2.5	2.7	2.9	3.1	23
24	0.2	0.4	0.6	0.8	1.0	1.2	1.4	1.6	1.8	2.0	2.2	2.4	2.6	2.8	3.0	3.2	24
25	0.2	0.4	0.6	0.8	1.0	1.2	1.5	1.7	1.9	2.1	2.3	2.5	2.7	2.9	3.1	3.3	25
26	0.2	0.4	0.6	0.9	1.1	1.3	1.5	1.7	2.0	2.2	2.4	2.6	2.8	3.0	3.2	3.5	26
27	0.2	0.4	0.7	0.9	1.1	1.4	1.6	1.8	2.0	2.2	2.5	2.7	2.9	3.2	3.4	3.6	27
28	0.2	0.5	0.7	0.9	1.2	1.4	1.6	1.9	2.1	2.3	2.6	2.8	3.0	3.3	3.5	3.7	28
29	0.2	0.5	0.7	1.0	1.2	1.4	1.7	1.9	2.2	2.4	2.7	2.9	3.1	3.4	3.6	3.9	29
30	0.2	0.5	0.8	1.0	1.2	1.5	1.8	2.0	2.2	2.5	2.8	3.0	3.2	3.5	3.8	4.0	30
31	0.3	0.5	0.8	1.0	1.3	1.6	1.8	2.1	2.3	2.6	2.8	3.1	3.4	3.6	3.9	4.1	31
32	0.3	0.5	0.8	1.1	1.3	1.6	1.9	2.1	2.4	2.7	2.9	3.2	3.5	3.7	4.0	4.3	32
33	0.3	0.6	0.8	1.1	1.4	1.6	1.9	2.2	2.5	2.8	3.0	3.3	3.6	3.8	4.1	4.4	33
34	0.3	0.6	0.8	1.1	1.4	1.7	2.0	2.3	2.6	2.8	3.1	3.4	3.7	4.0	4.2	4.5	34
35	0.3	0.6	0.9	1.2	1.5	1.8	2.0	2.3	2.6	2.9	3.2	3.5	3.8	4.1	4.4	4.7	35
36	0.3	0.6	0.9	1.2	1.5	1.8	2.1	2.4	2.7	3.0	3.3	3.6	3.9	4.2	4.5	4.8	36
37	0.3	0.6	0.9	1.2	1.5	1.8	2.2	2.5	2.8	3.1	3.4	3.7	4.0	4.3	4.6	4.9	37
38	0.3	0.6	1.0	1.3	1.6	1.9	2.2	2.5	2.8	3.2	3.5	3.8	4.1	4.4	4.8	5.1	38
39	0.3	0.6	1.0	1.3	1.6	2.0	2.3	2.6	2.9	3.2	3.6	3.9	4.2	4.6	4.9	5.2	39
40	0.3	0.7	1.0	1.3	1.7	2.0	2.3	2.7	3.0	3.3	3.7	4.0	4.3	4.7	5.0	5.3	40
41	0.3	0.7	1.0	1.4	1.7	2.0	2.4	2.7	3.1	3.4	3.8	4.1	4.4	4.8	5.1	5.5	41
42	0.4	0.7	1.0	1.4	1.8	2.1	2.4	2.8	3.2	3.5	3.8	4.2	4.6	4.9	5.2	5.6	42
43	0.4	0.7	1.1	1.4	1.8	2.2	2.5	2.9	3.2	3.6	3.9	4.3	4.7	5.0	5.4	5.7	43
44	0.4	0.7	1.1	1.5	1.8	2.2	2.6	2.9	3.3	3.7	4.0	4.4	4.8	5.1	5.5	5.9	44
45	0.4	0.8	1.1	1.5	1.9	2.2	2.6	3.0	3.4	3.8	4.1	4.5	4.9	5.2	5.6	6.0	45
46	0.4	0.8	1.2	1.5	1.9	2.3	2.7	3.1	3.4	3.8	4.2	4.6	5.0	5.4	5.8	6.1	46
47	0.4	0.8	1.2	1.6	2.0	2.4	2.7	3.1	3.5	3.9	4.3	4.7	5.1	5.5	5.9	6.3	47
48	0.4	0.8	1.2	1.6	2.0	2.4	2.8	3.2	3.6	4.0	4.4	4.8	5.2	5.6	6.0	6.4	48
49	0.4	0.8	1.2	1.6	2.0	2.4	2.9	3.3	3.7	4.1	4.5	4.9	5.3	5.7	6.1	6.5	49
50	0.4	0.8	1.2	1.7	2.1	2.5	2.9	3.3	3.8	4.2	4.6	5.0	5.4	5.8	6.2	6.7	50
51	0.4	0.8	1.3	1.7	2.1	2.6	3.0	3.4	3.8	4.2	4.7	5.1	5.5	6.0	6.4	6.8	51
52	0.4	0.9	1.3	1.7	2.2	2.6	3.0	3.5	3.9	4.3	4.8	5.2	5.6	6.1	6.5	6.9	52
53	0.4	0.9	1.3	1.8	2.2	2.6	3.1	3.5	4.0	4.4	4.9	5.3	5.7	6.2	6.6	7.1	53
54	0.4	0.9	1.4	1.8	2.2	2.7	3.2	3.6	4.0	4.5	5.0	5.4	5.8	6.3	6.8	7.2	54
55	0.5	0.9	1.4	1.8	2.3	2.8	3.2	3.7	4.1	4.6	5.0	5.5	6.0	6.4	6.9	7.3	55
56	0.5	0.9	1.4	1.9	2.3	2.8	3.3	3.7	4.2	4.7	5.1	5.6	6.1	6.5	7.0	7.5	56
57	0.5	1.0	1.4	1.9	2.4	2.8	3.3	3.8	4.3	4.8	5.2	5.7	6.2	6.6	7.1	7.6	57
58	0.5	1.0	1.4	1.9	2.4	2.9	3.4	3.9	4.4	4.8	5.3	5.8	6.3	6.8	7.2	7.7	58
59	0.5	1.0	1.5	2.0	2.5	3.0	3.4	3.9	4.4	4.9	5.4	5.9	6.4	6.9	7.4	7.9	59
60	0.5	1.0	1.5	2.0	2.5	3.0	3.5	4.0	4.5	5.0	5.5	6.0	6.5	7.0	7.5	8.0	60

TABLE VIII

Speed, Time, and Distance, *cont'd.*

Minutes	8.5	9.0	9.5	10.0	10.5	11.0	11.5	12.0	12.5	13.0	13.5	14.0	14.5	15.0	15.5	16.0	Minutes
	Speed in knots																
	Miles	*Miles*	*Miles*	*Miles*	*Miles*	*Miles*	*Miles*	*Miles*	*Miles*	*Miles*	*Miles*	*Miles*	*Miles*	*Miles*	*Miles*	*Miles*	
1	0.1	0.2	0.2	0.2	0.2	0.2	0.2	0.2	0.2	0.2	0.2	0.2	0.2	0.2	0.3	0.3	1
2	0.3	0.3	0.3	0.3	0.4	0.4	0.4	0.4	0.4	0.4	0.4	0.5	0.5	0.5	0.5	0.5	2
3	0.4	0.4	0.5	0.5	0.5	0.6	0.6	0.6	0.6	0.6	0.7	0.7	0.7	0.8	0.8	0.8	3
4	0.6	0.6	0.6	0.7	0.7	0.7	0.8	0.8	0.8	0.9	0.9	0.9	1.0	1.0	1.0	1.1	4
5	0.7	0.8	0.8	0.8	0.9	0.9	1.0	1.0	1.0	1.1	1.1	1.2	1.2	1.2	1.3	1.3	5
6	0.8	0.9	1.0	1.0	1.0	1.1	1.2	1.2	1.2	1.3	1.4	1.4	1.4	1.5	1.6	1.6	6
7	1.0	1.0	1.1	1.2	1.2	1.3	1.3	1.4	1.5	1.5	1.6	1.6	1.7	1.8	1.8	1.9	7
8	1.1	1.2	1.3	1.3	1.4	1.5	1.5	1.6	1.7	1.7	1.8	1.9	1.9	2.0	2.1	2.1	8
9	1.3	1.4	1.4	1.5	1.6	1.6	1.7	1.8	1.9	2.0	2.0	2.1	2.2	2.2	2.3	2.4	9
10	1.4	1.5	1.6	1.7	1.8	1.8	1.9	2.0	2.1	2.2	2.2	2.3	2.4	2.5	2.6	2.7	10
11	1.6	1.6	1.7	1.8	1.9	2.0	2.1	2.2	2.3	2.4	2.5	2.6	2.7	2.8	2.8	2.9	11
12	1.7	1.8	1.9	2.0	2.1	2.2	2.3	2.4	2.5	2.6	2.7	2.8	2.9	3.0	3.1	3.2	12
13	1.8	2.0	2.1	2.2	2.3	2.4	2.5	2.6	2.7	2.8	2.9	3.0	3.1	3.2	3.4	3.5	13
14	2.0	2.1	2.2	2.3	2.4	2.6	2.7	2.8	2.9	3.0	3.2	3.3	3.4	3.5	3.6	3.7	14
15	2.1	2.2	2.4	2.5	2.6	2.8	2.9	3.0	3.1	3.2	3.4	3.5	3.6	3.8	3.9	4.0	15
16	2.3	2.4	2.5	2.7	2.8	2.9	3.1	3.2	3.3	3.5	3.6	3.7	3.9	4.0	4.1	4.3	16
17	2.4	2.6	2.7	2.8	3.0	3.1	3.3	3.4	3.5	3.7	3.8	4.0	4.1	4.2	4.4	4.5	17
18	2.6	2.7	2.8	3.0	3.2	3.3	3.4	3.6	3.8	3.9	4.0	4.2	4.4	4.5	4.6	4.8	18
19	2.7	2.8	3.0	3.2	3.3	3.5	3.6	3.8	4.0	4.1	4.3	4.4	4.6	4.8	4.9	5.1	19
20	2.8	3.0	3.2	3.3	3.5	3.7	3.8	4.0	4.2	4.3	4.5	4.7	4.8	5.0	5.2	5.3	20
21	3.0	3.2	3.3	3.5	3.7	3.8	4.0	4.2	4.4	4.6	4.7	4.9	5.1	5.2	5.4	5.6	21
22	3.1	3.3	3.5	3.7	3.8	4.0	4.2	4.4	4.6	4.8	5.0	5.1	5.3	5.5	5.7	5.9	22
23	3.3	3.4	3.6	3.8	4.0	4.2	4.4	4.6	4.8	5.0	5.2	5.4	5.6	5.8	5.9	6.1	23
24	3.4	3.6	3.8	4.0	4.2	4.4	4.6	4.8	5.0	5.2	5.4	5.6	5.8	6.0	6.2	6.4	24
25	3.5	3.8	4.0	4.2	4.4	4.6	4.8	5.0	5.2	5.4	5.6	5.8	6.0	6.2	6.5	6.7	25
26	3.7	3.9	4.1	4.3	4.6	4.8	5.0	5.2	5.4	5.6	5.8	6.1	6.3	6.5	6.7	6.9	26
27	3.8	4.0	4.3	4.5	4.7	5.0	5.2	5.4	5.6	5.8	6.1	6.3	6.5	6.8	7.0	7.2	27
28	4.0	4.2	4.4	4.7	4.9	5.1	5.4	5.6	5.8	6.1	6.3	6.5	6.8	7.0	7.2	7.5	28
29	4.1	4.4	4.6	4.8	5.1	5.3	5.6	5.8	6.0	6.3	6.5	6.8	7.0	7.2	7.5	7.7	29
30	4.2	4.5	4.8	5.0	5.2	5.5	5.8	6.0	6.2	6.5	6.8	7.0	7.2	7.5	7.8	8.0	30
31	4.4	4.6	4.9	5.2	5.4	5.7	5.9	6.2	6.5	6.7	7.0	7.2	7.5	7.8	8.0	8.3	31
32	4.5	4.8	5.1	5.3	5.6	5.9	6.1	6.4	6.7	6.9	7.2	7.5	7.7	8.0	8.3	8.5	32
33	4.7	5.0	5.2	5.5	5.8	6.0	6.3	6.6	6.9	7.2	7.4	7.7	8.0	8.2	8.5	8.8	33
34	4.8	5.1	5.4	5.7	6.0	6.2	6.5	6.8	7.1	7.4	7.6	7.9	8.2	8.5	8.8	9.1	34
35	5.0	5.2	5.5	5.8	6.1	6.4	6.7	7.0	7.3	7.6	7.9	8.2	8.5	8.8	9.0	9.3	35
36	5.1	5.4	5.7	6.0	6.3	6.6	6.9	7.2	7.5	7.8	8.1	8.4	8.7	9.0	9.3	9.6	36
37	5.2	5.6	5.9	6.2	6.5	6.8	7.1	7.4	7.7	8.0	8.3	8.6	8.9	9.2	9.6	9.9	37
38	5.4	5.7	6.0	6.3	6.6	7.0	7.3	7.6	7.9	8.2	8.6	8.9	9.2	9.5	9.8	10.1	38
39	5.5	5.8	6.2	6.5	6.8	7.2	7.5	7.8	8.1	8.4	8.8	9.1	9.4	9.8	10.1	10.4	39
40	5.7	6.0	6.3	6.7	7.0	7.3	7.7	8.0	8.3	8.7	9.0	9.3	9.7	10.0	10.3	10.7	40
41	5.8	6.2	6.5	6.8	7.2	7.5	7.9	8.2	8.5	8.9	9.2	9.6	9.9	10.2	10.6	10.9	41
42	6.0	6.3	6.6	7.0	7.4	7.7	8.0	8.4	8.8	9.1	9.4	9.8	10.2	10.5	10.8	11.2	42
43	6.1	6.4	6.8	7.2	7.5	7.9	8.2	8.6	9.0	9.3	9.7	10.0	10.4	10.8	11.1	11.5	43
44	6.2	6.6	7.0	7.3	7.7	8.1	8.4	8.8	9.2	9.5	9.9	10.3	10.6	11.0	11.4	11.7	44
45	6.4	6.8	7.1	7.5	7.9	8.2	8.6	9.0	9.4	9.8	10.1	10.5	10.9	11.2	11.6	12.0	45
46	6.5	6.9	7.3	7.7	8.0	8.4	8.8	9.2	9.6	10.0	10.4	10.7	11.1	11.5	11.9	12.3	46
47	6.7	7.0	7.4	7.8	8.2	8.6	9.0	9.4	9.8	10.2	10.6	11.0	11.4	11.8	12.1	12.5	47
48	6.8	7.2	7.6	8.0	8.4	8.8	9.2	9.6	10.0	10.4	10.8	11.2	11.6	12.0	12.4	12.8	48
49	6.9	7.4	7.8	8.2	8.6	9.0	9.4	9.8	10.2	10.6	11.0	11.4	11.8	12.2	12.7	13.1	49
50	7.1	7.5	7.9	8.3	8.8	9.2	9.6	10.0	10.4	10.8	11.2	11.7	12.1	12.5	12.9	13.3	50
51	7.2	7.6	8.1	8.5	8.9	9.4	9.8	10.2	10.6	11.0	11.5	11.9	12.3	12.8	13.2	13.6	51
52	7.4	7.8	8.2	8.7	9.1	9.5	10.0	10.4	10.8	11.3	11.7	12.1	12.6	13.0	13.4	13.9	52
53	7.5	8.0	8.4	8.8	9.3	9.7	10.2	10.6	11.0	11.5	11.9	12.4	12.8	13.2	13.7	14.1	53
54	7.6	8.1	8.6	9.0	9.4	9.9	10.4	10.8	11.2	11.7	12.2	12.6	13.0	13.5	14.0	14.4	54
55	7.8	8.2	8.7	9.2	9.6	10.1	10.5	11.0	11.5	11.9	12.4	12.8	13.3	13.8	14.2	14.7	55
56	7.9	8.4	8.9	9.3	9.8	10.3	10.7	11.2	11.7	12.1	12.6	13.1	13.5	14.0	14.5	14.9	56
57	8.1	8.6	9.0	9.5	10.0	10.4	10.9	11.4	11.9	12.4	12.8	13.3	13.8	14.2	14.7	15.2	57
58	8.2	8.7	9.2	9.7	10.2	10.6	11.1	11.6	12.1	12.6	13.0	13.5	14.0	14.5	15.0	15.5	58
59	8.4	8.8	9.3	9.8	10.3	10.8	11.3	11.8	12.3	12.8	13.3	13.8	14.3	14.8	15.2	15.7	59
60	8.5	9.0	9.5	10.0	10.5	11.0	11.5	12.0	12.5	13.0	13.5	14.0	14.5	15.0	15.5	16.0	60

INDEX